D0276677

Mums

Mums

A Celebration of MOTHERHOOD

Edited by Sarah Brown and Gil McNeil

3 5 7 9 10 8 6 4

Published in 2007 by Ebury Press, an imprint of Ebury Publishing

Ebury Publishing is a division of the Random House Group

The Random House Group Limited Reg. No. 954009

Addresses for companies within the Random House Group
can be found at www.randomhouse.co.uk

A CIP catalogue record for this book is available from the British Library

The Random House Group Limited makes every effort to ensure that
the papers used in our books are made from trees that have been legally
sourced from well-managed and credibly certified forests. Our paper
procurement policy can be found on www.randomhouse.co.uk

Printed and bound in Great Britain by Mackays of Chatham plc

Designed and typeset by seagulls.net

ISBN 9780091910662

Contents

Mums

Introduction

I adore short stories; they are the perfect way to immerse yourself in another world for a limited time. Looking after two small children and working with a number of charities, as well as the various demands of life at 11 Downing Street, means I don't always have as much time to read as I would like; but I often manage to grab time to read a story on a train journey or over a sandwich lunch at my desk. As you can imagine, editing this book has been a dream since it has involved working with so many of my favourite authors, and being able to look forward to new stories and personal recollections arriving in the post or by email each week.

All parents will immediately understand how the highs and lows of being a mum are like nothing else you ever encounter, and make other experiences pale into insignificance. Parenthood has also made me re-evaluate and appreciate better all that my mother did for my family while we were growing up, something that clearly strikes a chord with many of the contributors to this book. So it seems entirely appropriate to celebrate motherhood as the theme for this book, our fifth anthology for the children's charity, PiggyBankKids.

Since I launched PiggyBankKids in 2002 we have supported a range of innovative charitable projects, including the Jennifer Brown Research Fund, which supports a medical research laboratory based at the Royal Infirmary in Edinburgh, seeking solutions to pregnancy and birth problems. We have also worked on a wide range of partnership projects with other charities, including improving sports provision for children with learning difficulties, providing cancer care for teenagers, and mentoring matches for vulnerable school children.

Thank you so much for buying this book and helping us to raise funds to support all our projects. I'd like to thank my co-editor, Gil McNeil, and everyone at Ebury and PiggyBankKids for all their hard work. Most of all, I would like to thank all our marvellous writers and artists who have so generously agreed to contribute their work for free. And of course last, but not least, thanks to all our mums.

Sarah Brown
PiggyBankKids

'When they were young I urged them to move on to the next step: talking, walking, reading, writing. Now they're 19 and 23 I'd give anything to roll them back a bit and constantly wonder where all those years went. My advice is to savour every step – even the paddies, door slamming and loud music – they're gone all too soon and you don't half miss them!'

Jenni Murray

Under the Acacia

Alexander McCall Smith

'Your mother?' said Mma Ramotswe. 'You said something about your mother? I was not paying attention, Mma Makutsi. I missed what you said.'

The two women had been in the van, driving out of Gaborone, out to a village where they had to speak to somebody about somebody who was missing. It was a hopeless case; people went missing all the time because they wanted to, not because somebody had abducted them or lured them away. They simply went missing because they had had enough. Of course one had to make an effort in such cases. One could hardly say to the client, 'Look, this person has gone away because he can't stand your nagging any more.' You could not say that; you had to try to find some trace, so that a mind could be set at rest. The worst thing, Mma Ramotswe thought, was not to know. It was not easy not to know.

Now, halfway through the journey, along a broken road that had to be negotiated very slowly, they stopped under a tree by the side and ate the sandwiches which Mma Makutsi had packed for them – thick slices of bread, roughly cut, with slices of ham and tomato between them. Mma Ramotswe liked ham, but she thought that it was spoiled by tomatoes and she wondered whether she could tactfully extract the tomato and drop it on the ground beside her – food for ants. But she decided that she could not, as Mma Makutsi would notice and that was just the sort of thing that could lead to offence being taken. Mma Makutsi took offence; not often, but she took it.

'You said something about your mother,' Mma Ramotswe repeated. 'I was thinking about food, I'm afraid – about these fine sandwiches and I didn't hear what you said about your mother.'

Mma Makutsi's mouth was full, and she had to wait until she had swallowed before she could reply. 'I said that she did not like dust. I said that if there was too much dust her eyes would water and she would be very uncomfortable.'

'An allergy,' said Mma Ramotswe.

Mma Makutsi nodded. She had a piece of ham stuck in between her teeth, at the front, and she tackled this, turning her head away as she did so. 'Yes, an allergy.'

'This is not a good country if you're allergic to dust,' observed Mma Ramotswe, looking down at the ground beneath them. They were sitting on a couple of rocks under the tree – rocks which other people had left there for people to sit on – and there was fine, sandy soil underfoot, and dust. There was dust everywhere, and when you drove along a road such as this the dust followed you in clouds like a vapour trail. Even her tiny white van, the least of machines, so modest, so old, had a vapour trail like that of a jet.

'That is why she liked the rainy season,' Mma Makutsi said. She had extracted the fragment of ham and she let it fall to the ground, a tiny speck, lost in the desert sand.

'Do you remember much about your mother?' asked Mma Ramotswe. 'How old were you when she became late?'

'Oh, I remember her very well. Very well. She only became late a few years ago.' She stopped and thought. Four years. That was all. But at least she had known about the graduation from the Botswana Secretarial College, about the ninety-seven per cent; she had known about that and had been so proud, as the whole family was.

'Ninety-seven per cent?' she had said. 'I cannot believe it. Ninety-seven per cent?'

'Yes.'

That had been such a proud moment, after all the sacrifices that the Makutsi family had made to put their daughter through the college; the livestock sold so that the fees could be paid, the meals that she was sure they had missed so that she could buy the books that she had needed. There had been no complaint about any of that; it had simply been done, because that was what family meant. They were poor – when she had been asked by her father to fill in some government form for him, something to do with a grant for a water pipe, he had instructed her to write *peasant* in the box which said *occupation*. The form had been in English, and that was the word that he wanted to use. She said, 'What about *farmer*?' and he had shaken his head and said, 'I like *peasant*. That is what I want to be.'

Mma Makutsi looked at Mma Ramotswe. She had heard a lot about her employer's father, Obed Ramotswe, but not much about her mother. Obed Ramotswe had been a great man, by all accounts, and not just in Mma Ramotswe's estimation – she regularly heard comments from others who had known him, and they were all complimentary. Mma Makutsi could imagine him, this man who had brought up Precious Ramotswe, with his old hat and his eye for cattle. She smiled at the thought. But then she turned to Mma Ramotswe. 'And your mother?' she asked.

Mma Ramotswe was silent.

'It's just that I have heard so much about your father,' Mma Makutsi went on. 'But I have never heard about your mother. I know that she is late, but you never talk …'

Mma Ramotswe put the remains of her sandwich on her knee and reached for the bottle of water they had brought from the van. Above them, in the delicate foliage of the acacia tree, she could make out the remnants of a bird's nest, a sad bundle of twigs. There was a gecko on the branch below the nest, one of those small, brightly coloured creatures that scampered up the trunks of trees, unworried by gravity; unlike us, she thought, for whom gravity was always there, and such a problem sometimes.

'No,' she said. 'I don't talk about her very much.'

Mma Makutsi was watching her. She saw the familiar, comfortable figure of her employer; saw the purple-dyed dress that she liked to wear when she went off on investigations, the scarf tied about the head like one of those *doeks* which the Herero women liked to wear. What would somebody, some stranger, make of this woman whom she so took for granted? Would a stranger be able to tell what sort of woman she was? There is so much that we do not know about other people, she thought; we imagined we knew about them, but we did not, not really. Often we knew only what they wanted us to know, and the other things, the things that were really very interesting, were kept hidden. She wondered about Mma Ramotswe, and any secrets that she might be concealing; but then she thought, no, there are no secrets there. And then the further thought came, that she had no secrets herself, which was a depressing conclusion, that one's life should have no secrets, not even a few.

Why, she wondered, would Mma Ramotswe not wish to talk about her late mother? Sometimes people did not like to talk about those who were recently late – the just late – but Mma Ramotswe's mother had died a long time ago, when Precious was a child. It was not a recent loss.

'What was she like, Mma? What was your mother like?'

Mma Ramotswe retrieved her sandwich from its resting place on her knee. She looked up at the sky. 'I was very small,' she said. 'I was just a baby. She was killed in an accident on a level crossing – you know that one near Pilane? You know that place?'

Mma Makutsi did. She was regretting now that she had asked Mma Ramotswe about this. It was obviously a painful topic.

'We don't know how it happened,' said Mma Ramotswe. 'The train had a light. How can you not see a train? How can you not hear it?'

'Sometimes people don't,' said Mma Makutsi. 'It can be very dark. The light of a train – that light on the front – might seem like the moon, don't you think? And the noise – if it's the rainy season you might think that it's a storm. There are many reasons ...'

There were; but some of these reasons were not so easy to live with. 'Maybe.'

'So you don't remember her, Mma? You have no memories?'

Mma Ramotswe shook her head. 'I do not remember her.'

'That is very sad.'

'I do not think about it, Mma. I do not think about it.'

Mma Makutsi reached for the bottle of water. It seemed to her to be strange that Mma Ramotswe should not think about her mother; would it not be better to think about her at least a little bit, to find out from others, perhaps, as to what she was like? It seemed odd, almost unnatural, to allow a gap like that to exist, an area of unknowing.

'Maybe ...' Mma Makutsi began, but she was interrupted by Mma Ramotswe, who said, 'Yes, maybe I should. But then how can I talk about something I know nothing about? How can I do that, Mma?'

'Somebody must have spoken to you about her,' said Mma Makutsi. 'They must have said something.'

'No,' said Mma Ramotswe. 'I don't think they did. I think it was too hard for my father to speak about her. His heart was broken inside him, you see. That is why he could not speak.'

Mma Makutsi frowned. 'Never?'

'Not ever that I remember ... except ...'

Mma Makutsi leaned forward and touched Mma Ramotswe lightly on the forearm. 'You remember something, don't you, Mma?'

Mma Ramotswe hesitated. She was not sure. It was a long time ago. But he had said to her, had he not, that she was like her mother? He had said it once when she was a young woman, seventeen or thereabouts, and she had come back to Mochudi from a visit to an aunt and had found her father standing by that stone wall that ran near their house. It had been in the evening, and he had been standing there, staring out over the field, and she had come up to him to give him a surprise. He had heard her, had spun round, smiled, and said, 'You are just like your mother, you know. She had a dress like that, Precious, and you look like her. I thought ...' He trailed off, and her breath had caught within her, as she imagined that he was going to say more, but the moment passed and he did not.

She told Mma Makutsi this, and the younger woman had smiled at her with encouragement. 'There you are, Mma Ramotswe,' she said. 'I thought that you knew something after all. So we know that she was just like you. Does that not make you happy?'

Mma Ramotswe shrugged. 'I don't know. Aren't we all like our parents? And aren't they all like us?'

Mma Makutsi thought for a moment. She had known many people who struck her as being very different from their parents, for which they, and many others too, were very grateful. There was that young man, also from Bobonong, the one who almost married her cousin; his father was the headmaster of a school, but that young man ... well, it was best not to think about him. But it was different with Mma Ramotswe – very different, and she would have to tell her that. It was a bit embarrassing, perhaps, but she would have to tell her.

'But listen, Mma,' she said. 'It's a very good thing to

be like you. I would be very happy if I were like you. I really would.'

Mma Ramotswe made a gesture of embarrassment. 'No,' she said. 'You must not say things like that! I am just the same as anybody else.' She looked at Mma Makutsi, who had lowered her gaze, and at this point, surreptitiously, almost on impulse, she deftly slipped a slice of tomato out of her sandwich and flicked it down on to the ground. Then, with a quick movement of the foot, she covered it with her shoe.

'But that is not true!' said Mma Makutsi. 'It is just not true. You are a very nice woman, Mma Ramotswe. Everybody likes you. You are kind. You never shout at anyone – even those stupid apprentices. No, you don't. I have never heard you raise your voice to them. I have done that myself. Yes, I have. But not you.'

Mma Ramotswe said nothing. She thought that Mma Makutsi was rather impatient with those young men, even if they did offer frequent provocations, but she did not think it was necessarily productive to shout at people. But now, she felt, was not the time to say that; not immediately after being showered with such praise.

'So you know a lot about your mother, Mma Ramotswe,' Mma Makutsi continued. 'You know that she was kind. You know that she was very pretty ...'

'And traditionally built,' interrupted Mma Ramotswe.

'Maybe. Maybe. But you know that people must have liked her a lot. She would have been popular in Mochudi. Many people would have been at her funeral, you know.'

'Yes,' said Mma Ramotswe. 'There were a lot of people. I heard that once – from an old man, a distant relative. And somebody else told me that too.'

'There you are,' exclaimed Mma Makutsi. 'You know a lot about her, Mma. Can you not see her now?'

Mma Ramotswe looked out beyond her tiny white van, which was parked to the side of the tree under which they were sitting. 'I think she would have liked my van,' she said. 'I can see her driving that. I can see her driving up towards the *kgotla* at Mochudi, with a cloud of dust behind her.'

'And dogs running after the van and barking,' suggested Mma Makutsi. 'I can see that too.'

Mma Ramotswe smiled. 'And I think that she would have been very kind to me,' she said.

Mma Makutsi was silent for a moment. She had been looking up, through the leaves of the acacia tree, at a sky which the leaves split up into fragments of blue, of white, of emptiness. 'She would have loved you so much,' she said. 'And you would have loved her too.'

Mma Ramotswe turned to face her. 'Can you love a person you cannot remember, Mma? Can you do that?'

Mma Makutsi replied without a moment of hesitation. There was no doubt in her mind; none. 'Yes you can, Mma. Of course you can. Of course.'

'I see.'

They sat for a few minutes more, under the shade of the tree. Somewhere, off in the bush behind them, there were cattle bells, and it seemed enough for them that they should listen to that familiar sound of the Botswana bush, a sound which reminded them of who they were, and where they were. Then Mma Ramotswe stood up. It was so comfortable on that smooth rock, but there was a journey to be completed.

'We must go, Mma,' she said. 'We have work to do.'

Mma Makutsi stood up too. She reached for the water bottle. Then Mma Ramotswe took a step towards the van and saw, as she did so, that the slice of tomato, rejected and lying in the white dust of that place, was very visible.

Mma Makutsi did not appear to see it, and they went over to the van, brushing their skirts to get rid of fragments of sand; a dusty place. Once in the van, Mma Ramotswe started the engine and they drove, bumpily, back onto the road. She was thinking of what her assistant had said. It had been very good of her, very helpful.

'What you said back there,' said Mma Ramotswe, slowing down to avoid a donkey that had strayed into the road and was gazing mournfully, almost accusingly, at the sudden appearance of the van. 'What you said back there, Mma Makutsi, was very kind. Thank you. You are very kind.'

Her companion nodded, somewhat curtly, thought Mma Ramotswe.

'Even if you didn't like my sandwiches,' muttered Mma Makutsi.

'Every time I cook, I think about my mother. I may cook different things, but I cook in exactly the same way: impatiently, greedily, with stubborn confidence. I enjoy cooking more than she did; and I am always aware that referring to mothers in the kitchen conjures up a false domestic idyll. My mother belied the contemporary belief that good food is cooked with love. She cooked wonderfully, but often the pans were clattered about with resentment and tension, and she was impatient, often to the point of hysteria, with us her kitchen slaves.

But when she cooked for herself, she was calm. Her two favourite meals were cabbage, a huge pile of it, doused in butter and sprinkled with caraway seeds, and fierce grindings of white pepper, and bread and milk; both of which she ate out of cracked cream pudding basins. The bread and milk is the ultimate evocation of her food, and the smell of vanillery milk is enough to conjure up the picture of her, shiny faced with baby lotion, which she always smeared all over herself after a bath, and barefooted, sitting on a strange velvet-covered rocking chair, clasping her bowl to her. This is how I make it:

2 fat slices good white bread, slightly stale is fine
2 teaspoons sugar, or vanilla sugar
250ml milk

Tear the bread into chunks and put into a bowl, sprinkling with the sugar. If you're not using vanilla sugar, add a drop of vanilla essence to the milk and heat it in a pan until warm, but not hot. Pour over the bread and sugar and eat, although 'eat' sounds too active for the sort of activity required to ingest this, the perfect comfort food: no chewing, just warm, wet carbohydrate.'

Nigella Lawson

Matchmaker, Matchmaker

Meera Syal

'Oh darling … I'll get the malted milks …'

Asha sat a sobbing Kavita down at the kitchen table and made straight for the novelty biscuit tin in the shape of a smiling pig wearing a chequered waistcoat. As she lifted its head off, the disembodied porker emitted a loud oink and told her in a slightly sinister electronic voice that she was 'Naughty girl! Who's pigging out?' Asha grabbed a handful of the caramel-coloured rectangles with their edged borders and delicate raised outline of a grazing cow, always Kavita's favourite since she was small, and shut the lid quickly, remembering the row, years ago, with her daughter about the 'Woman-hating, body-hating piece of tat that you decided to keep the bloody biscuits in!'

She had been quite upset the first time Kavita had laid into the pig. Asha had thought it was both cute and functional, as who didn't dip their hands into the biscuits unthinkingly when watching television? And besides, as she painstakingly pointed out, she, Asha, had not actually bought the pig: it had been a gift from a former pupil who made such novelty items in his very successful business, and it was the thought, as always, that counted. But the tactless pig proved to be just the first in a long list of things that made Kavita angry over the years. At first it was big general things, subjects that would indeed make any right-minded person with a conscience angry: global warming, war, third world debt, animals becoming extinct. The teenage Kavita, all hair, limbs and baffling mood swings, would stomp about the kitchen throwing newspapers in exasperation on the table as yet another article told her that the world she was growing up in was sad, cruel and doomed. Some days Kavita would burst out into hot tears of fury and embarrassment, break down at the table over the photo of an emaciated child in a desert, so wasted that it seemed the sun had merely reduced a real child to a charred, splintered stick. Then Asha would take Kavita in her arms, smelling the strange hormonal odours emanating from what used to be her little girl; where she used to inhale soapy sweetness and vanilla, just at the nape of her neck, there was now a musky dampness that made Asha think of secrets and caves and it made her feel unsettled and, maybe, just a little afraid.

Then during Kavita's university years, the outbursts became less frequent but more measured, the targets more specific: American foreign policy, the situation in Burma, female infanticide in Rajasthan, genital mutilation in the Sudan. It was as if Kavita was on some strange world tour which poo-pooed such fripperies as the Eiffel Tower and the Parthenon and went straight for the crisis zones where she disembarked as a warrior tourist, ready to save all who needed her. At such times, Asha would sit benignly at the table and let Kavita declaim as she gulped down mouthfuls of hot, home-cooked Punjabi food, wondering how many calories Kavita burned up as she exploded with passionate outrage and whether all these marches she seemed to attend were affecting her grades.

Her girl was passionate; oh, she knew that from the start, a fierce babbling baby who would sometimes bat away Asha's breast to tell her mother about some ongoing indignity in her milky universe. Asha, to occupy herself, would often put words to Kavita's nonsensical babbling, as if she was waving a pudgy fist on a platform at some baby demonstration. 'Dad a bad a!' burbled Kavita. ('Toddlers of the world!' thought Asha …) 'Bbbrbr ba ba …' ('… I say to you … !') 'Ma-ma-ppfft …' ('… how long must we suffer … the indignity … of having our nappies changed in front of complete strangers … who happen to visit the house?') Kavita would resume suckling for a moment, then a new thought would flit across her moon-round face, the breast would be heaved aside and another gummy diatribe would follow, Asha amusing herself quietly, adoring her daughter's vitality, envying it. Kavita was so like her father, the man she chose to marry against her

Boobs? I Hadn't Noticed … I can't even get dumped in an original way. What's wrong with me?'

'Nothing, darling. It's not you, it's … I mean, he's the idiot. At least you only wasted six months on him. Not like …' Asha bit her lip. She hadn't meant to mention Dev.

''S OK, Mum. Wasted years. You're right. Four years on Dev, who went off with a blonde because I must have been Too Indian or maybe reminded him too much of his mother … so then I assumed an English bloke would treat me better because some of them love Exotic on their arm, but I was wrong again.'

Kavita paused, wiping her eyes on the sleeve of her suit. Asha itched to hand her a tissue, they were just nearby, but instead took Kavita's hand in hers. It was warm; her fingers trembled slightly in Asha's palm.

'I'm running my own company, my friends say I'm pretty and funny …'

'You are. Really.'

'Mum, here's the reality. I've been dating since I was seventeen. I'm nearly thirty-five, the age when my ovaries will officially start shrivelling up. I've eaten tapas with geeks, mummies' boys, Peter Pans, shag-arounds, sandal-wearing socialists, alpha male go-getters from virtually every continent, every height, shade, weight and income bracket. I haven't, you know … been with them all, but neither have I been … unrealistically … fussy …'

No, You Bloody Haven't, thought Asha, her face

getting warm. How had she fitted in so many dalliances without Asha knowing? All the chats around this table, all the hard work she put into being Modern Mother, never judging, always listening, and now this. Did she know her own daughter at all? She glanced over at Rajesh's photo. His grin seemed to have slipped slightly off his face. He looked disappointed. For a brief white flash of a second, she felt like picking up the photo and flinging it against the wall.

'You should have arranged my marriage.'

Asha thought she heard wrong. She smiled warmly, squeezing Kavita's hand.

'You, Mum, you should have arranged a marriage for me. When everyone else's daughter was doing it. Oh, I don't mean in the way it's always reported in the press, virgin hitched to goat-herder second cousin. I mean the way your friends did it – families meet, I date someone's son for a while, and we hit it off or we don't.'

Asha swallowed. 'But …'

'There's no time wasters, Mum. You both know why you're there. No game playing, no will he call/commit/propose/move in? You've background-checked him, you see if you've got chemistry and you take a leap of faith. I've done all those things when I've met a bloke in a bar. Except there's no safety net. No one to tell him, move on or get out. That's where parents come in. I mean, you're not going to mess a woman around when you know two sets of families are expecting you to behave with … honour. God, listen to me, I sound like some Tory matron from the Home Counties. But I can't think of another word that describes what modern men don't have any more, Mum. Honour.'

Asha cleared her throat. When she spoke, her voice sounded strained, unfamiliar.

'You've really thought about this, haven't you?'

'A lot. Recently.' Kavita sighed and broke off the corner of a malted milk biscuit, toying with the crumbs. 'Between me and my friends, we've tried every dating method invented, pubs and clubs, speed dating, Internet matchmaking, singles' dinners, agencies and friends of friends' little black books, going to Tesco's late night Thursdays …'

'Tesco's?'

'Demographically when most single men do their shopping. And yes, there's men out there but …'

A long pause. Asha swore she saw, out of the corner of her eye, Rajesh's photo shift half an inch across its shelf.

'But I can't do it on my own any more, Mum, I'm tired. Now it's your turn. You find the men, I'll give it a go. I trust your judgement. After all, you found Dad, didn't you?'

A sharp pain zigzagged across Asha's forehead. She got up, a little too quickly, and had to steady herself against the table before she went over to Rajesh's picture and checked its position. In the faint sprinkling of dust – she hadn't cleaned this shelf for at least a week and chapatti flour gave everything in this corner a faint snowy tinge – she saw the drag marks of the serrated frame. Half an inch. Maybe more. She moved the photo back, then, after a moment's hesitation, placed the frame face down gently.

'What was that for?' Kavita asked, a grin curling her lips.

Asha sat down again. She spoke quickly, almost in a whisper, almost as if he could hear her.

'I had only known your father three years when he died. Three months of courtship, the rest in marriage, and with you coming along so quickly … well …'

'Well what?' Kavita looked worried, as if Asha might now blame her for intruding upon the fairy-tale marriage she had constructed in her head, to fill the gap left by a father who had only ever been a photograph for most of her life.

'I didn't know him very well really.'

'Some people say you never know anyone properly until you live with them. But you knew enough to agree to marry him, didn't you?'

'We were found out so quickly, we had to make a decision quickly, to marry or not, no living together business then. There was so much pressure suddenly … we would have looked … foolish then to change our minds.'

Kavita's face had fallen now. Unbearably for Asha, she looked about three years old, bewilderment opening and softening her face, still hoping for the Happy Ever After.

'Why would you have wanted to change your minds? Didn't you love him?'

Asha stared at her daughter; how beautiful she was, and how fragile, her *patake*, her firework child, whose loud, optimistic displays threw into dark relief Asha's own small cautious world. Kavita believed every problem had a solution, that it was merely a question of trying different strategies until something shifted, or resolved. Asha did not see problems or solutions: she just accepted the good and bad equally, some kind of buried genetic pragmatism which made her a placid woman, but also, she now realised for the first time, a lazy one too. If all is prewritten, if all is meant to be, then why bother to try and change anything? Would changing paths midway still lead you inevitably to your fate, waiting there, at the end of the road you thought you chose with such spontaneous abandon? Whenever anyone asked, she always said that she had married Rajesh because it was Inevitable. Now, she wondered, was that merely an acceptably romantic way of saying she couldn't be bothered to say Wait? What kind of message was that to give to her bold, beloved girl?

'Of course I loved him.'

Kavita's shoulders relaxed.

'But blind love isn't enough. It's also ...'

'Working at a relationship, mutual respect, time out to talk, blah blah blah ... Mum, I know all that. I know we might not find anyone right out there, especially 'cos I'm a bit past the Indian sell-by date and all that ...'

'Not nowadays! Renu Aggarwal's daughter got married last month – she's thirty-six! Mind you, it was his second time round so ...'

'So being old, she was palmed off with shop-soiled goods ...'

Asha hesitated, and watched the giggle build in Kavita's chest and bubble from her mouth. Asha laughed too.

'You're so easy to wind up, Mum!'

Kavita offered a biscuit to Asha and they both munched in companionable silence for a while.

'Someone like me, Indian roots, watered in British soil, loves the food and language, hates the fundamentalists and hypocrites ... someone you'd want in our family. Someone you think is good enough for me.'

Asha glanced over at Rajesh's photo. She should turn him over again really. He wasn't here. She was.

'Mrs Sharma's son, I hear, has just become single. Ajay. They are a very lovely family ...'

'And if I don't like him, if he's a moose-face or picks his nose or has Mummy issues ...'

'We look for someone else. Plenty of fishes in the ocean.'

Kavita laughed for the first time, throaty and full, which made Asha smile.

'Right, Mum. Plenty.'

Shirley Hughes

Two Mothers

Rosamunde Pilcher

My mother was born in the Orkney Islands, one of eight children, the offspring of a hardworking farmer and his wife. When she was in her teens, they fell upon hard times; I suspect a drink problem on the part of my grandfather, but this was never confirmed. The farm was sold and the family moved to Glasgow. All the boys and one sister emigrated to the United States, so only three sisters were left. Davina married a doctor, domiciled in the wilds of the Western Highlands. The second sister, Nan, married a dear man who had been a sergeant in the Argyll and Sutherland Highlanders during the First World War. His job was in Glasgow and they lived in a wonderfully cosy tenement house with a washing line in the communal yard, and a parlour kept for when the minister came to call.

My mother married my father. He was an officer in the Royal Navy, and I can only imagine they met while his ship was in port. No details were ever shared with us. Whatever, they became engaged, and my mother travelled alone to Hong Kong, where they were married in Hong Kong cathedral and spent a two-day honeymoon in Kowloon. My father left the Navy and they moved on to Australia, where he thought he would make his fortune farming. This did not happen and they were forced to return home, my father selling his gun in order to pay for the passage. By now there were three of them, my older sister having been born in 1919 in Turramurra.

I think this was probably the first time my mother met her in-laws, and the encounter was not successful. His family considered, not perhaps without justification, that their eldest son had married beneath him and were appalled that my sister, now aged five, spoke with a strong Australian accent. My mother never truly forgave them for this initial rejection, and there was always a certain frigidity in the air on the few occasions when they all got together. Much of this emanated from my mother, which was sad, because I only remember affection and welcome from these various aunts and uncles and would have loved to see more of them and spend time with my cousins.

Life was not easy after the First World War and jobs were hard to come by. Finally, my father was offered employment, but it was in Burma, working for the government. He was put in charge of the Irrawaddy dredging works in Rangoon harbour, keeping the river port open for boats, laden with teak and rubies, that sailed down from Mandalay. It was a responsible job and he was housed accordingly, in some style. My mother, pregnant with me, did not accompany him. Alone, she cast about for some place to live, to bring up two children. She settled for Cornwall, where once she had visited a girlfriend. Weighing up the pros and cons, she decided that if she was going to have to bring up two children on her own, she might as well do it in a pleasant place.

We ended up in Lelant, on the Hayle estuary and only three miles from St Ives. At first she stayed in a small boarding house, where I was born with the help of the village midwife, and then we took possession of a rented house, The Elms, where we remained until 1939 and the Second World War.

Being without a father was not unusual in those days. Most families seemed to have some male or other out in India, or Malaya, or Africa, planting rubber, or doing their bit to keep the British Empire ticking along, or serving in the armed forces. Having never known my father, I did not miss him, but it must have been very hard for my sister. At five years old, she knew my father well: he was one half of her family. When he went to Burma, he virtually left for good, doing stints of three or four years before getting three months' home leave. Air travel was in its infancy, and the P&O boats took three weeks to make the long journey through the Indian Ocean, the Suez Canal and the Mediterranean. There was no telephone connection, and in an emergency the only form of contact was a telegram. He wrote to us every week, a letter each, neatly typed and we wrote back, but for a small girl, missing him desperately, it must have been traumatic. Her reaction to this loss was to bury herself in books. She had learned to read very early, and losing herself in her book was her refuge from the day-to-day trials and disappointments of life. This escape route, like a drug, remained with her until the day she died, at fifty-two, of cancer in Sausalito, California.

I suppose we were friends, but seldom played together. Sometimes on a wet morning, we would go up to the nursery and indulge in her favourite flight of fancy, dressing up in grown-up clothes and pretending that my father was coming home. The attic staircase was the train to London; the spare bedroom, the docks; the landing was the gangway, where we waited for him to make his way down from the upper deck of the P&O liner.

Her other passion was dancing. We both went to dancing class, and my sister took to the occasions like a duck to water. She was forever pirouetting and doing arabesques, and tried hard to be the teacher and pass her passion on to me. I hated dancing. I have always been uncoordinated and singularly unsupple, and I galumphed miserably about in the beginners' class. Our teacher was called Miss Fildes. She had red hair and my sister was deeply in love with her.

What I really wanted was to be taught to play piano. We had an old upright in our winter sitting room, and I was hugely frustrated by the knowledge that music lay behind the ebony-black wood ... music that only needed a little knowledge to release it. I found an old book of student songs and taught myself to pick out the tunes with one finger, but never progressed any further.

If my father had been around, I am sure he would have recognised my desire, cancelled out the dancing classes and started me on piano lessons. But my mother could be very unperceptive, and maybe this was deliberate because the hassle of dancing class, the expense, the logistics of actually getting us there was just about all she could deal with.

Another void in the normal pattern of family life was created by the fact that my mother, for reasons that I have never understood, had decided, at some point, to embrace Christian Science. I would not recommend any parent to lumber his or her children with this arrogant doctrine. For us, it meant that we never went to the pretty, ancient village church, built on the edge of the golf course and within sight of the sea. I was, actually, christened there, but that was the only time I was taken, formally, through its doorway. And if we were ill, running temperatures, or choking with whooping cough, we were simply told to think beautiful thoughts. Christian Science dictated that we never experienced the kindly masculine presence of either local priest or family doctor, and it was seldom that a man of any sort came through our front door.

Because of this, I was fascinated by them and made friends with the most unlikely people. The coalman, delivering coal on his horse-drawn cart. And Willie, who had a little pony and a float, and brought trunks and suitcases up the hill from the station when there were guests from London, come to stay at one of the big houses. And if a workman turned up to fix a dripping tap, or do a bit of painting, I drove him mad with my constant companionship and endless questions.

Despite all this, I was perfectly happy. Because my sister was not very companionable, I learned contentment on my own, or else played with one of the boys next door. There were few restrictions. I played in the garden, and then opened the gate, and moved on to the lane, and the little station, and the pinewood. And then, over the railway line, and down to the shore of the estuary. The changing tides were an endless diversion.

As we grew older, we went to the big beach. My mother did not come. She disliked sand and chill sea breezes. But there was always a small group of beach-goers gathered by the church, and we'd join up with them, a straggling cavalcade of babies in pushchairs, visiting teenagers, dogs and nannies, and sometimes an intrepid parent or two. We took our own picnic tea in a basket, and it was at this time that I learned that sad truth, i.e. other people's picnics are always better than one's own.

Meantime, my mother lived her own life. She was an accomplished seamstress and always busy creating a dress, or a pair of curtains, or cotton frocks for her two daughters. Up to a point, she was quite social. A tea party, perhaps, and a little sedate mah-jong. Her friends were inclined to be the village eccentrics, but there were ex-Burma colleagues as well, now retired and living nearby. Otherwise, she was not a great entertainer, although the boys next door and their friends and cousins always enjoyed coming to our house for tea. Because my mother loved to bake, there were always piles of scones and cakes and pancakes for hungry boys to wolf down.

In summertime, sometimes friends would come to stay, or rent out the house next door to us, while the neighbours took themselves off to London for a month, to enjoy hotel life and a little urban distraction. Our favourite family were the Gilberts, Irish and totally unpredictable. Henry Gilbert had been in the Navy with my father. He had four lively daughters and a Scottish wife, who never did anything but sit by the fire, write letters and eat peppermint creams. They were a noisy and demonstrative lot and I loved it when they were around, because there was always laughter, and huge, soft hugs, and someone to give a piggyback if your legs were tired.

We seldom went away from home, because living in Cornwall was a bit like being on holiday all year round.

Lovely things were all about us. The Atlantic Ocean, the white beaches and the wind-blown dunes. The little golf links, aromatic with the scent of thyme. The long summers; the short, gale-torn winters; the miraculously early springs. The train ride to St Ives, along the very rim of the cliffs, and then shopping in the steep, narrow streets of the town. The presence, everywhere, of artists, potters, writers, sculptors. The magic of surfing on belly boards on Porthmeor beach, or doing the cliff walk, all three miles of it, on cold, grey winter afternoons. The moors inland and Trencrom hill, where grew the earliest of the wild primroses. The green parkland of Trevethoe, where lived Jiffy Tyringhame, our squire, and where the church fête took place every summer. And our own little village, with its grocer, butcher, sweet shop, post office and pub. The smell of violets, the scent of flowering privet and the spicy tang of escallonia. And always the salty freshness of the sea and the dull thunder of distant rollers breaking up on the shore.

We went to school. I did lessons with the vicar's wife, and my sister went to St Clare's in Penzance. When I was eight, I followed her there, and on my first day decided that I must have a special friend. I picked a sturdy little girl, with dark bobbed hair and a fringe. We danced the polka together, accompanied by a tinny piano. At the end of the day, I caught the bus home and burst into the house to tell my mother. 'I have a best friend.'

She laughed. She always thought me something of a joke.

'It's true,' I insisted.

'Just wait till tomorrow, and see if she still likes you.'

'She will.'

And she did. Sarah Trembath remained my friend all my life, until she died.

And her mother, Kitty Trembath, became my second mother.

Jim Trembath was the manager of Lloyds Bank in Penzance, that handsome domed building that stands, like some Florentine church, at the top of Market Jew Street. The Trembaths were Cornish farmers who, at some time, had left Cornwall and moved to Gloucestershire. This move had involved a large herd of cattle, and all the Trembath menfolk, however young, had been involved in this massive drive. Jim was the second son, so the Gloucestershire farm was destined for his older brother, and Jim was put to work with Lloyds Bank. He prospered, married, had his two little girls and was working as manager in a small town in Derbyshire when he was offered the post in Penzance.

He moved to Cornwall. The family moved into a white stucco, early Victorian villa between Penzance and Newlyn. It had spacious walled gardens sloped down the hill, and ... give or take a tall terrace of dour houses smack in the way ... a prospect of Mount's Bay.

Jim was a passionate gardener. His farming blood and his love of growing things was fulfilled by his garden and every weekend, and every summer evening, he was out there, working in his old clothes, trimming and staking and weeding and watering. He grew peaches, trained up the high wall, and pollinated them with a rabbit's scut on a long pole. And there were pears as well, and a cucumber frame, and spectacular sweet peas. He had an old greenhouse which always smelled of freesia, and a noisy motor mower which he drove to and fro, cutting the grass on the extremely cramped tennis court, so that we could put up the net and have a game.

He had a car as well, an old Austin with a dickey, but this stayed in the garage (an old coach house) all week, for he always walked the mile or so to work, striding out, spare and trim, rain or shine, with his shoes polished and a flower in his buttonhole. On summer Sundays, the car would come out and we would all pile in and go for picnics to Rinsey, or Prussia, or Porthcurno, or Treen. Or drive across the narrow width of the county to Portheras, the cove hidden far below the massive north cliffs.

He read aloud better than anyone has ever done, putting on a different voice for all the characters, but always sounding as Cornish as he was. He read us *Tarka the Otter*, and we all blubbed, and he read *Treasure Island* but we found Blind Pew so scary that he had to stop and hide the book away.

At night, when we were asleep, he would come upstairs and leave us each a toffee by our beds, to be chewed and relished first thing in the morning.

Harriet, Sarah's sister, was two years older than Sarah and myself, but because of her sweet nature and natural friendliness, there was never any friction among the three of us. She was a clever, diligent child, always top of her class, and good at everything. She even sang in the school choir. I was very fond of her, and wished that my own sister could be so cooperative, instead of her constant insistence that I was too stupid for words.

Their mother, Kitty Trembath, came from South Wales. When I first met her, she must have been in her late thirties, a sweet-faced woman with a smile that made her beautiful. She smiled a lot, and from our very first encounter I was made to feel special, as though I was the one person she really wanted to see. The house was her responsibility, with the considerable assistance of a living-in cook (Hilda) and a house parlour maid (Eileen). Even in this modest set-up, a nanny would have been the norm, but Kitty loved her daughters too much to hand them over to another person.

Theirs was an old house and nobody had ever thought to modernise it. Quite shabby and well worn, it smelled of floor polish, with a faint whiff of antique shops which I found delightful. Surprisingly, it had been built with a lavatory, complete with rose-patterned bowl, a cistern and a chain. But no bathroom. It had, however, a charming curved staircase which led to the upper floor, and some previous owner had hit upon the bright idea of building a bathroom on to the turn of this staircase, where once a large and ornate window would have let the light in. This bathroom was simply a wooden extension tacked on to the back wall, over the kitchen yard, and propped in position by a couple of sturdy posts. In winter it was very cold, and I always expected it, one day, to come away from its moorings and crash down on to the washing line.

But it never did.

Downstairs, there was a drawing room, a dining room, a morning room and the kitchen. The kitchen was wonderfully archaic, with a Cornish range for cooking and a huge scullery at the back. The morning room was given over to the children, not a nursery, but a sitting room with sagging sofas and books on shelves, and a fire which, in winter months, was always lighted and blazing away by the time we had finished breakfast.

My first visit to the Trembaths was a Saturday in November, when I was invited by Sarah to go for lunch. I travelled to Penzance by bus, a bundle of nervous excitement. Would the Trembaths like me? What would I be given to eat, and what would I do if it was Brussels sprouts? Would I be shown, right away, the location of the lavatory? What would happen if I lost my return bus ticket?

But all was well. Mrs Trembath and Sarah were waiting to meet me at the last bus stop and, for a marvellous moment, I thought Mrs Trembath was going to embrace me. We walked to their house and there was the gardener, digging in the vegetable patch. The gardener turned out to be Sarah's father. Lunch was in the dining room, the table formally laid. It was mutton stew and cauliflower, so that was all right. And there was jelly for pudding.

We spent the afternoon out of doors, and playing hide and seek. I realised that there was space for every sort of game, and the bonus of a trellised summerhouse smothered in prickly roses, and a huge chestnut tree. When it grew dark, we came indoors for tea, and it was time to go home again. Mr Trembath walked me to the bus stop and saw me away, and I travelled home in a bliss of remembrance, wondering how soon it would be before I was asked again.

By the time I got to Lelant, night had fallen. Alone, I walked home down the dark country road, unlit by street lamps, and the bare branches of November trees swayed in the wind high above me and the wind smelt of salt. I began to run, because it was cold and I wanted to be safely home and to tell my mother every single detail.

She was amused by my excitement.

'What a time you've had.'

'I hope they'll ask me again.'

'I shouldn't count on it.'

But I was sure they would. And they did.

Over the months, I became one of the Trembath family. Harriet and Sarah were the companionable sisters I had never known, and before long I was invited to call their parents Uncle Jim and Auntie Kitty. During the Easter term, when Cornwall is at its most glorious, I was asked to spend the half-term holiday, all four days, from Thursday to Tuesday.

My excitement was unbounded. I had never been away to stay by myself before, but on the Thursday morning set off for school with my satchel and my week-end bag, and without a backward glance. As for my mother, she had new sitting-room curtains to be stitched, a border to be weeded and a mah-jong tea party organised; and she was probably quite pleased to have me out of the way. And as for my sister, she had become more involved than ever in her books and her school work and her dancing classes. A display was being organ-ised by Miss Fildes, and my sister yearned to be given the part of Columbine in a little ballet and, when not lost in some book, could be found practising at the barre (the upstairs banister) or sticking pictures of Irina Baranova up on her bedroom wall.

Living with the Trembaths, having my own bedroom, coming down to breakfast in the mornings, was a satisfying experience. The weather was spring-like, but even if it poured with rain, Auntie Kitty was a reli-able source of entertaining ideas and would produce a packet of transfers, or three new painting books, with promises of a prize for the best colourist. The prize was probably a toffee, or a little bar of Nestles chocolate, but in the end we all got one because she was tender-hearted and upset by disappointed faces.

Life was not lavish. There were no expensive treats, even at Christmas time, but Auntie Kitty had a flair for thinking up absorbing ploys or making the dullest of walks into an exploration or an adventure. She had a total rapport with children, and I am convinced that she preferred our company to unsympathetic grown-ups.

In the drawing room, there was a grand piano. She was not particularly accomplished, but quite capable of playing a tune for musical bumps or accompanying the three of us, should we be impelled to sing, with rollicking choruses of 'Blow Away the Morning Dew' or 'Sweet Lass of Richmond Hill'.

As well, there was a wireless, which was more than we had at home, and we listened regularly to *Henry Hall and His Orchestra* and *In Town Tonight*, which was one of the earliest chat shows. Sometimes, on Saturday evenings, there would be an operetta to listen to – *The Merry Widow* or *Wild Violets* – and on these occasions Auntie Kitty made a little event of it, turning down the lights and pretending we were in the theatre, the firelight the footlights and a small box of Cadbury's Milk Tray to hand round in the 'interval'.

She was a pious person and her Anglican faith meant a great deal to her. She liked to go to church on Sunday mornings and sometimes we went with her, walking the length of Penzance promenade and up the steep street to

St Mary's. The services were very High – classic smells and bells – with Sung Eucharist and incense being flung about, and it was always a relief to get out into the fresh air again, and walk home to the cheerful prospect of Sunday lunch.

It was some time before my mother and Auntie Kitty met each other. The encounter was not a rousing success, because my mother had become slightly jealous of my devotion to this unknown woman; and because Auntie Kitty found it impossible to forgive my mother for her Christian Science.

When I told her about this, innocently blurting it out, Auntie Kitty was deeply affected. She felt, with some justification, that my spiritual and physical needs were being neglected and I think from that moment on her feelings for me were both altered and deepened. I was not simply a school friend of Sarah's, but vulnerable and needy and she longed to keep me with her for ever, and mould my life into the ways that she felt my future should follow.

I was aware of this conflict between my two mothers, but chose to ignore it. Divided loyalties are difficult at the best of times, and at ten years old impossible to deal with.

When I was twelve, my sister, at seventeen, left school and my mother decided to take her out to Burma for a year, to grow up and to spend some time with my father in his house in Rangoon. I would be left on my own. At first it was decided that I should board at St Clare's and spend holidays with any person willing to have me. I did not think this was at all a good idea, and neither did Auntie Kitty. She swallowed her pride, telephoned my mother and said, please, please, could I spend the year with the Trembaths. I could go to school each day with Sarah and Kitty, and Uncle Jim promised that they would take the greatest care of me.

My mother bucked slightly at this scheme. Perhaps she felt that she was simply handing me over, giving me away to another family. And she had always hated decisions or control being taken out of her hands. At first, she declined the invitation, but then my father intervened: letters passed to and from Burma, and finally, to my enormous relief, my mother gave in and agreed to the plan.

Trunks were packed and passages booked. My mother's sewing machine became red hot, whizzing away at tropical dresses for the two of them. Then it was time to say goodbye, and they disappeared, borne away by the London train. Auntie Kitty was with me to see them off. When the train had disappeared, we walked from the platform and through the booking office, and out on to the car park where the old Trembath Austin waited for us.

That year, without my family, flew by, terms and holidays and seasons crowding in on each other. The three of us walked to school in the morning, and home again at four o'clock, in time for tea and then to do our homework. Auntie Kitty was very firm about this, and believed that homework should be dealt with at once, so that we could light-heartedly enjoy what remained of the evening. Homework was always a hurdle, but Auntie Kitty was prepared to help, which my mother never would. She did not do the work for us, but was always there, producing a dictionary or an encyclopaedia if needed, or hearing our French verbs, or testing history dates. She was useless, however, at maths, and we all spent hours struggling over algebra and sadistic problems. Trying to divide four pounds, eight shillings and four pence by one pound, two shillings and six pence caused us all much grief and frustration, and although we got good marks for all our other work, Sarah and I both trailed miserably when it came to maths.

In the Easter holidays, we went on primrose-gathering expeditions and if it was anything like warm enough, insisted on bathing in the sea. In and out of the breakers, just for a frozen moment, and then scurrying up the beach, blue with cold, to be bundled into warm sweaters and given a ginger biscuit which was meant to alleviate the agony.

At one point, we all got measles together and the doctor came to inspect our spots and take our temperatures, and cheer us on our way.

In summer, the garden baked in a heatwave, and the

tennis court dried out and flowers blazed from the borders. We lay in the shade, in a grassy corner where Uncle Jim kept his roller, and read books until it was cool enough to walk down to the rocky little beach below the house and have an evening swim. One summer morning, we got up tremendously early and walked down to Newlyn to watch the French crabbers come into harbour and unload their catch. As the summer died, we picked blackberries for Hilda to make bramble jelly, and took picnics up on to the moors, where the bracken turned gold and heather bloomed in great cushions of purple.

And then it was Christmas, and the house was transformed, with sparkly lights and home-made paper chains. Uncle Jim brought home a tree, and this was set up in the hall, to be hung, by us, with time-worn decorations, angels and robins and glittering balls, and tinsel, unravelled from the depths of a cardboard box. The turkey was supplied by some grateful farming client of the bank, and Hilda made Christmas puddings and cakes, and the kitchen was filled with the delicious scents of rich baking.

All this was magically new to me. My mother, brought up in the far north of Scotland, had never seriously celebrated Christmas, and was not about to start now. She never bothered with a tree, insisting that it made too much mess, and if you put up holly, you just had to take it down again. And so I specially enjoyed the secrecy of wrapped parcels and forbidden cupboards, and the pleasure of buying presents for everybody, and finding my own hiding place, and then handing them out on Christmas morning.

The year was nearly over. In February my mother and my sister returned from Burma and I was taken back to Lelant and reunited with them. It could have been difficult, but I had grown up a lot, had found my own personality and my own confidence. I abandoned Christian Science and refused to attend the colourless meetings in the Christian Science reading room in St Ives. And I no longer bothered about my sister's acerbic remarks as to my appearance, because I had grown taller and slimmer, and had discovered I was not stupid, and, if I wanted, could make people laugh.

In a strange way, it was good to be home again, like slipping on an old and familiar pair of shoes. And I discovered how much I had missed being on my own from time to time, and the luxury of solitude.

On my first free day back in Lelant, I went out for a long walk, checking on childhood haunts and making sure that nothing had changed. Which it hadn't. I walked by way of the railway line, and the old sea wall, and the grubby little beach where defunct fishing boats had been pulled up on to the shingle and left to rot. I crossed the golf links and climbed up on to the dunes, and saw the huge beach, pristine at low tide, the horizon flat and blue, and the houses of St Ives just visible in the distance. And it was bliss to be on my own, with my own thoughts and nobody to chat or to tell me what they wanted to do.

It was perhaps the end of childhood. Harriet was sent off to boarding school, and Sarah followed her a year later. A war was coming, although we all still hoped that it wouldn't. My sister went to London to get a job of some sort. When the war finally started, she joined the Women's Royal Naval Service, and when I had finished school and learned how to type I followed in her footsteps.

Auntie Kitty stayed close to me and remained one of my dearest friends. Uncle Jim died when he was seventy, but she stayed on in the old house, active as ever, busy with her garden and the church, and her bridge games, and, in time, with her six grandchildren. I grew up and married and had children of my own, and every year took them back to Cornwall. Once, shopping in Penzance, I spied Auntie Kitty striding along, weighed down by two laden carrier bags. I stopped the car, and we hugged and I asked her what she was doing and she told me. 'Just taking some runner beans to those poor old things in the old folks' home.' And probably most of the poor old things were at least ten years younger than she was.

She lived to a ripe old age and when she died Harriet and her husband moved into the house where we had all been so happy. And after another decade or so, Harriet's daughter and *her* family took the property over. I am sure it will continue thus for at least two more generations.

As for my own mother, I stayed loyal to her. Pretty, capable and amusing, she was as well moody, stubborn and sometimes downright untrustworthy. But it was she who, in the first place, brought us to Cornwall, and if it had not been for this inspired decision, none of what I have written would ever have happened.

And so, always, I remain grateful to her.

‘I had the most wonderful mother in the world. She was exquisitely beautiful, extremely funny, endlessly kind, incredibly well read and she also had an amazing capacity for friendship and one of the most crowded address books of anyone I’ve ever met. My abiding memory of her was rushing back to the drawing room after lunch and curling up on the floor or in an armchair and devouring another fifty pages of Kingsley Amis or Jane Austen or Anthony Powell, before she did anything else. She taught me about wild flowers when we went for walks. She taught me to adore animals. The only time I ever saw her cry as a child was when I came back from school to be told that Jamie, our Scottish terrier, had died.

She was adored by her grandchildren. She was a wonderful role model of what a wife should be: loving, cherishing and deeply, staunchly loyal.

Later in life, my mother had a great gift for malapropism! I remember one early July afternoon her ringing up and saying, "Oh darling, darling, isn't it wonderful, Virginia Woolf's just won Wimbledon."

She was always terrified of being a nuisance to the family when she got old. She never was. She lived in a little flat in Brighton and had millions of friends and used to come and stay with us in Gloucestershire; she never demanded a colossal amount of attention, but she was such good company, people wanted to give her attention.

She was in pretty good health until the day she died at the age of ninety-two. The night before she died, she rang her secretary Linda, saying she didn't feel well and thought she ought to go to the hospital. While she and Linda were waiting for the ambulance, my mother said how extraordinary life was and that about seventy years ago an aunt had left her an upright piano and, with the money, she told Linda, she went skiing in Switzerland for the first time. In the party was her boyfriend Hilary, who promptly fell in love with another member of the party called Marjorie. My mother was very sad for a day or two, then suddenly she noticed Bill, my father, who was very, very handsome and had eyes bluer than the sky and always seemed to appear over the horizon every time she fell over in the snow. By the end of the holiday she was madly in love with him, and they got engaged.

Then my mother went on to tell Linda: "I had two children, Timothy and Jilly, who I love very dearly, and they all had children and so I've got lots and lots of lovely grandchildren. I had such a happy marriage to Bill and have had such a happy life, and all thanks to one little upright piano." My mother then went to hospital, had a heart attack and died the following morning. Although I was terribly sad that she didn't regain consciousness except to squeeze my hand, I thought it was a lovely way to go: being grateful for so much happiness. It was just a great privilege to have known her.'

Jilly Cooper

Well Drilled

Penny Vincenzi

The minute Joanna saw Angie she knew she didn't like her. She had no reason to know that, since Angie was smiling at her in a very friendly, charming way, had paused in her raffle-ticket selling, indeed, and was standing up, holding out her hand to her and saying, 'You must be Daisy's mum. How lovely to meet you. Kate talks about nothing but Daisy these days, about how clever she is, and how good at gymnastics and all that sort of thing, and how she wants to have her to tea. So we must arrange that before the evening is out.'

And before Joanna could say yes, that would be a good idea, Angie had turned her attention to Laurence, and was saying goodness, you must be Daisy's dad, we've heard all about you, and how you're a photographer, I mean, goodness, how glamorous is that. What you're doing here at our little quiz night, goodness knows, when you could be with all those supermodels, have you actually ever met Kate Moss ...'

How could women still be like that, Joanna thought;

it was so old-fashioned, all that buttering up men and fluttering your eyelashes at them, so sixties – or was it seventies or eighties? Anyway, certainly not the way to behave now. And Angie was dressed for the activity too, in a black clingy top, cut low to show off a pair of beautifully shaped brown breasts, and white trousers that clung to every curve of her irritatingly narrow hips …

The enraging thing, of course, was that the men liked being buttered up, they never saw through it, never saw how foolish they looked, how totally uncool as the children would say, drooling in response as Laurence was now, saying it wasn't quite those sort of photographs he took actually, more landscapes and cityscapes, working with and for architects, and that no, he hadn't met Kate Moss although of course he'd love to, and …

'Well, welcome anyway. It's lovely to have you here. Now you're on table nine – let's see, yes, lots of nice people there, why don't you go over, introduce yourselves …'

The evening was fun; and as an ice-breaker it certainly worked. Joanna left the school hall with several phone numbers, and Laurence had been invited to join the squash club.

'That was really great, wasn't it?' he said as they walked home. 'I think we'll very soon feel we belong here, don't you?'

'I do,' said Joanna, and that was actually the first night she didn't lie in bed feeling homesick for

Edinburgh where they had lived for the past ten years, ever since they'd been married.

Daisy was longing to hear about it next morning: '… and did you meet Kate's mum, and did she say about me going to tea?'

'Yes to both questions,' said Joanna, 'and I think we've agreed on next Tuesday. Um – does Kate have a dad?'

'Well, she does, but they're divorced,' said Daisy, 'and Kate only sees him at the weekend.'

'That's a shame,' said Joanna.

'Oh, no, Kate says she likes it that way, she gets loads more presents and stuff and he takes her anywhere she wants every Saturday.'

'I see,' was all Joanna said. So Angie was a divorcee. Talk about walking cliché …

Things seemed to be going well. Daisy seemed very happy at her new school, and Joanna made good friends with a couple of the mothers. A woman called Caroline, particularly, she liked; she had three children, and Rachel, who was in Daisy's class, was the oldest.

'So, how are you settling down?' asked Caroline over coffee the following week. 'And more importantly, maybe, how is Daisy?'

'She's very happy. And I think we're settling pretty well, thank you. Everyone's been really kind. Daisy has made lots of friends, specially Angie's daughter, Kate.'

'Oh really?' said Caroline. 'You want to be a little bit careful of that one. Very manipulative ...'

'I think I can see that. So, tell me about Angie,' said Joanna carefully, 'she seems very nice.'

'Not nice,' said Caroline briskly, 'lots of things – clever, organised, stylish, marvellous cook, but not nice. She's a complete cow actually, I really don't like her. She was all right till her husband left her, but now she is the archetypal predatory female. I mean, you saw how she was dressed the other night, was that really suitable gear for a quiz night—'

'The men liked it,' said Joanna.

'They certainly did. But it's lock up your husband time when she's on the prowl. Certainly yours, he's quite a dish, isn't he?'

'Not bad,' said Joanna cheerfully. 'I like him anyway.'

For a few weeks everything was fine; then Daisy came out of school one afternoon looking rather flushed and grabbed Joanna's hand.

'Can we go quickly?' she said.

'Of course. What's the matter?'

'Oh – nothing.'

Joanna realised that a group of little girls, including Kate, were all staring at Daisy and whispering to one another. She wondered what on earth might have happened; some quarrel, probably, that would blow over. Kate and Daisy had been thick as thieves yesterday.

Over tea, Daisy suddenly started to cry. 'I hate her,' she said, 'I really hate her.'

'Poppet, who?'

'Kate. She's so horrible.'

'But Daisy, you said she was your best friend.'

'Well, she's not any more. She's horrible.'

Joanna digested this. Then 'OK,' she said, 'in what way?'

'She's having five friends this Saturday, to take to the cinema, and then they're going to Pizza Express. With her dad. It's because she's got all As in her tests. And she spent a day deciding who to take. She kept writing notes to everyone, saying I might take you and I might not. How horrible is that?'

'Very horrible. Did she write you one of these notes?'

'Yes. But then she wrote another, saying she wasn't taking me because I didn't have proper clothes for it.'

'Proper clothes?' Joanna stared at her, quite shocked. 'What sort of proper clothes?'

'Well, like she wears. She's got so many, you know, trousers and leggings and long skirts and all that. And she says for the cinema everyone's got to look really cool. Wear boots. Leather boots, long ones, you know. And she knows I haven't got any ...'

'Darling,' said Joanna, 'that is completely beastly. I've never heard anything so horrid.'

'I know. And then she started whispering and writing more notes, only not to me this time, and they all started staring at me and giggling, and after school no one would speak to me. It was so horrible, Mum.'

'Of course it was. Little beast. Is Rachel going to this exclusive gathering?'

'No. She certainly hasn't got any leather boots. She's hardly got any nice clothes.'

Her voice, as she said this, had just a dusting of scorn on it. Joanna stood up.

'Daisy, that is not the sort of talk I like. You'll be as bad as Kate if you don't look out. Now what I suggest is, you ask Rachel for tea on Saturday and I'll take you both somewhere really nice. How would that be?'

'Cool,' said Daisy, managing a smile, 'thanks, Mum.'

Caroline was delighted that Rachel and Daisy were friends. 'She's poison, that Kate, I did warn you. She did something similar to Rachel last term. I tried to tell myself I should be sorry for her, her parents being divorced, but myself wouldn't listen.'

'I'm sure it'll blow over,' said Joanna easily.

But it didn't.

'Kate's playing cat and mouse with Daisy,' she said to Caroline a few weeks later. 'One day she'll be her friend, the next she won't. And she won't with a vengeance, it seems, gets all the others not to speak to her either.'

'I hope that doesn't include Rachel,' said Caroline.

Joanna said she didn't think so, but she knew it did,

sometimes. Rachel was a gentle child, and no match for the manipulative Kate. Kate knew Rachel was Daisy's friend and she was determined not to allow it.

Joanna had discovered what Daisy had done to deserve this warfare; it was because Daisy had landed the part of Cinderella in the school play. Kate had wanted to be Cinderella, very badly; and being cast as the fairy godmother hadn't mollified her in the least.

'She'd be better as one of the ugly sisters,' Kate said, in a loud voice that morning in the playground. 'Have you seen the size of her feet?'

Daisy did have big feet; big feet and very skinny legs, which made them look even bigger. But she did have a talent for acting, and a very good singing voice which had won her the part. Kate could dance rather well – and indeed attended classes in ballet, modern and tap – and had been told she would be doing a solo as the fairy godmother. But it wasn't enough; she was seething with jealousy and rage.

She became increasingly unkind to Daisy, whispering constantly behind her back, not allowing her to join in the playground games she organised, and worst of all, as Christmas drew nearer, announced she was going to have a party and that everyone would be invited.

'Everyone except her,' she whispered to her cohorts, indicating Daisy, 'she thinks she's so wonderful and she can't even do the polka. Did you see her at rehearsals with the prince, falling over those great feet of hers … ?'

Nobody quite knew why she had such power over the other children. Mrs Parsons, the form teacher who had observed some of it, discussed it and the trouble it caused with the other teachers.

'She has a very strong personality and she's established this clique, and everyone is quite literally afraid of her. I've seen it before, many times.'

'Have you discussed it with the mother?' asked Jim Lee, the headmaster.

'I've tried. Didn't get very far. She said Kate had been damaged by the marriage break-up and was very vulnerable. More or less accused me of being hard on her.'

'Well, I suppose that's possible. But I don't like it. If it gets any worse, let me know. I'll ask the mother to come and see me.'

'You'll enjoy that, won't you, Jim?' said Mrs Parsons tartly.

Daisy was so upset about not going to The Party, which had now become a giant ice-skating expedition, that Joanna decided to take matters into her own hands. She rang Angie one morning, said she knew she was speaking out of turn, but that Daisy was terribly upset about being the only child not invited to Kate's wonderful party, and could she beg an invitation for her.

'I'm sorry to hear this,' said Angie, sounding genuinely concerned; Joanna's heart lifted. 'And of course I hadn't realised.'

'So ...'

'But you know, I always think it's better for children to fight their own battles, be encouraged to stand up for themselves. It makes things worse in the long run if we interfere.'

'So – you won't help? Daisy is literally crying in bed every night.'

'Poor little soul. It's hard growing up, isn't it? I really can't, Joanna, I'm sorry. We've hired two minibuses and they're both full. I had no idea, obviously, that Daisy had been left out in this way.'

'We could bring her in the car,' said Joanna, desperation beginning to show in her voice. God, this was agony! The things you did for your children ...

'Look,' Angie said, suddenly sounding harder, 'this party isn't a charity, you know. It's for Kate and the friends she wants to invite. I don't want to force someone on her she doesn't want. She's earned it doing so well in her tests. I'm sorry, Joanna, but the answer has to be no. After all, Daisy's moment will come, won't it, in the pantomime? Think how Kate's going to feel that night ...'

So that's it, Joanne thought, she's jealous too; she's taking her own revenge.

'You know what?' Angie said. 'Next term they'll probably be best friends again and it'll be someone else left out. It's just how little girls are, I'm afraid.'

'I hope for your sake it isn't Kate,' said Joanna, and put the phone down.

*

On the day of the party, Joanna and Laurence took Daisy out for tea at the Pizza Express after school, but it felt all wrong, a very solitary, friendless outing. She was rather quiet and afterwards she said she had a tummy ache; next morning she said she didn't feel well enough to go to school.

Joanna knew why; she couldn't face everyone talking about the party.

But the pantomime was a great success; Daisy was really very good as Cinderella, everyone said so.

'She's got real talent,' Caroline whispered, as the curtain came down. 'You must be so proud.'

Joanna couldn't speak for the lump in her throat.

Afterwards there was a small party organised by the PTA. Angie was at full throttle, dressed in a black dress with no back, and not a lot of front. She came over to Joanna and Laurence, and clasped their hands.

'She was wonderful. You must be over the moon with pride. What a little star.'

'Thanks,' said Laurence. His eyes probed Angie's bosom.

'Now, I wondered if I could ask you a huge favour, Laurence.'

'Ye-es?'

'I want some really special pictures taken of Kate. Well, Kate and me together. Not just any old stuff. I was going to someone in Knightsbridge, but then I thought of you and I thought it would be much nicer if we had them done at home, rather than in some impersonal studio. How would you feel about that?'

'Well – I'd – be delighted of course, but—'

'I'm sorry, Angie,' said Joanna coolly, 'that really isn't Laurence's scene. He doesn't do people, do you, darling? Just buildings. Now, we have to go and help Caroline with the sausage rolls.'

It was hard to say who gave her the dirtier look, Angie or Laurence.

Afterwards Laurence was very irritated.

'What's wrong with the woman? She was lovely to us about Daisy, and it might have helped the situation between her and Kate if I'd done the pictures.'

'Laurence,' said Joanna, 'when were you born? I could have sworn I saw you around before yesterday.'

Christmas came and went; the respite from bullying made Daisy feel better, and the school got a rave review of the play in the local paper, with a special mention for 'a very talented Cinderella'.

'I think I'm going to go back to work,' Joanna said, as they took down the decorations on twelfth night. 'I've got the house sorted, and I'm getting a bit restless. There's a practice locally looking for someone. Best in the area, everyone says. Most of the people we know go to it. What would you think?'

'I'd think it was a great idea,' said Laurence, 'especially if they paid you.'

Joanna gave him a kiss.

'They probably will.'

The school term started quite well; Joanna had worked hard all over the holiday, entertaining children, trying to get some really good friendships going. Daisy was greeted quite warmly at the gates by several little girls, and came home that night cautiously cheerful.

'It's much better, Mummy. Kate's just ignoring me. I don't mind that. And Rachel and me are going to start a dancing club.'

'What a good idea,' said Joanna.

Maybe it was going to be all right; maybe they had turned the corner.

Half the class joined Daisy's dancing club; the sitting room becoming a studio once a week seemed a small price to pay.

'So, are you looking forward to going back to work?' Caroline said. 'I do envy you.'

'Think so, yes. Bit scared, of course. But the hours are fantastic; I can get home in time for picking up most days, and it'll be nice not to feel my skills rusting away. I'm going to do a refresher course, anything medical changes all the time.'

'I s'pose so. So what do we call you?'

'Dr Smithies. I'm working under my maiden name, to go with all my certificates and so on.'

'I shall call you Dr Joanna.'

The name caught on at the school gates; Dr Joanna she became.

They were three weeks into the term when Daisy came home in tears.

'I hate her so much,' she said.

'Who?' said Joanna.

'Kate, of course. She went round everyone in my club and said she was starting one, and everyone who joined would get a party bag after it every week.'

'Well – surely they can belong to both?'

'No, she won't let them. I really hate her, Mum.'

'I think I do too,' said Joanna.

She went to see Mrs Parsons. Mrs Parsons said carefully that she was aware that there was a problem with Kate and she would see what she could do.

Whatever it was, it made matters worse: Kate told Daisy she was a telltale tit. Joanna had never felt so helpless.

'It's so awful,' she said to Laurence. 'I just don't know what to do. Pair of bullies, they are, Kate and her mother.'

'I know. Cowards too, I expect,' he said. 'Bullies always are.'

'Of course. But how does that help me?'

*

Joanna was tidying up the surgery after her session two days later, when the receptionist buzzed her.

'Dr Smithies, I've got one of Dr Lane's patients on the phone. She says she's in really bad pain. As Dr Lane's away, I wondered if you could see her?'

'I really don't think I can,' said Joanna. 'I'm just leaving. What's her name?'

'Mrs Duke. Mrs Angela Duke.'

'Well, do you know – I think I could just about fit her in.'

Joanna was standing with her back to the door, sorting out one of her drawers, when Angie came in; she didn't turn or even look up.

'It is good of you to see me, Miss Smithies,' Angie said. 'I really am in the most hideous pain, I think it must be an abscess.'

'Oh dear,' said Joanna, 'well, let's have a look, see what's going on. Do make yourself comfortable in the chair, Mrs Duke.' She turned round, very slowly, and smiled sweetly at Angie – whose own smile had chilled on her face.

'Joanna!' she said. 'What a lovely surprise. I didn't realise you were a dentist! I thought you were a doctor when they were teasing you the other day—'

'Oh, no,' said Joanna. 'Dentists are all called doctor these days.'

'Mr Lane isn't.'

'No, well, he's one of the old school, isn't he? Now

what sort of pain is it? A dull ache, or does it throb? Does it wake you up at night? Show me where it hurts.'

'Here,' Angie prodded a tooth with her finger. 'I lost a piece of filling last night and …'

'Hmm. Let's see. Just give it a little tap.'

'Ouch! God, that hurts. Look, I'd better tell you right away, Joanna, I'm a bit of a coward about dentists. Mr Lane always gives me a very strong injection, even to do a check-up. Well, almost. Otherwise I might just run away.' She laughed nervously.

'I can't believe that. Doesn't sound like your philosophy, Angie. I seem to remember you saying it was better to – what was it? – face up to things. No, I don't think that's an abscess. I'll just drill this filling out and replace it. It'll be fine in no time.'

'Yes. Good. But—'

'Let's put these rather stylish glasses on, shall we? There. Open wide.'

She switched on the drill; Angie's eyes were wide with terror.

'Stop it,' she said, 'just stop it. You haven't given me any – any …'

'Novocaine? Honestly, I don't think it's necessary,' said Joanna, 'the nerves are completely dead. The tooth's been root filled. Now I'll just begin and if it does start to hurt, all you've got to do is put up your hand. I usually stop then. Only joking.'

*

Next day Daisy came out of school, radiant.

'Guess what?' she said.

'What?'

'Kate says why don't we run a dance club together. I can be in charge one week, and her the next. And she says she's sorry she's been mean to me, and next time her dad takes her somewhere really special, I can go too.'

'Well, isn't that nice?' said Joanna.

'What do you think's changed her mind, Mum?'

'I have no idea,' said Joanna, 'but you know, sometimes something makes people see they're being mean and decide to stop.'

'How was your day, Mum? You still glad you went back to work?'

'So glad,' said Joanna.

'I once met a very grown-up woman whose husband was a very grown-up and hugely important businessman. They had three children and she had spent the last twenty years as a full-time mother working to make her children happy – to achieve their potential – to be healthy, inspired, academically thriving, emotionally cogent, physically strong, thoughtful, caring, wonderful people. That year her eldest daughter was expecting her first child, and one Sunday evening the whole family had been discussing parenting. She had asked them what part of their upbringing had meant the most to them.

And every one of her children
had said that, much as they had appreciated it, it wasn't the organic food, the great schools, the tennis lessons, the holidays in the Mediterranean, the extra tutoring which enabled them to get into good universities,

the birthday presents, the well-cooked Sunday lunches or the bedtime stories. It wasn't the fact that their sports clothes were always ironed and ready, that their father had dressed up as Santa Claus when he delivered their stockings, or the home-made birthday cakes. Instead, they said it was the day, roughly once a year, when their mum, as usual, got them dressed for school, packed their lunchboxes, made sure they had their gym kit, homework and pencil case, got them into the car – and then just drove them all down to Brighton for a day on the beach. No warning, no preparation and no reason.

Before leaving, she would ring the school and say that all three children had come down with a tummy bug and wouldn't be in today but she was highly optimistic that it would have cleared up by the following morning. And they had played on the beach, had lunch in a café, gone on the dodgems, bought ice creams, built sandcastles and returned home. No point, no consequence, just because she could. And that was the best thing about their youth … their grown-up mum, in her sensible shoes, playing truant once a year, just for the hell of it.

After that conversation, I've tried to go on being a good mum – but slightly more often, I've tried to be a deliciously bad one.'

Emma Freud

The Light of the World

Kate Atkinson

Naturally, it never even crossed her mind. As far as Pam was concerned she was well into menopause – the 'change' as the members of her peer group (fellow teachers, Pilates class, book club) delicately referred to it, as if they were undergoing a metamorphosis into new creatures. 'Oh, but we are, we are,' a flushed Fiona G. said, spilling red wine all over her copy of *The Time Traveller's Wife* (not to mention Pam's newly dry-cleaned sofa covers). 'We shall spread our wings and fly!' she exclaimed with a gaiety that sounded vaguely hysterical to Pam's ears, although the other women smiled and nodded in agreement.

The 'change' had left the collective members of the book group giddy with possibilities ('HRT!' Fiona W. whispered excitedly when Pam caught her in Sainsbury's with a basket full of tampons, as if menstruating was a triumph of character over biology). Pam considered asking if any of them would like to test their new-found pinions by jumping off her roof into the damp spring air of suburban Edinburgh. She wondered when it was exactly that she had stopped being a nice person. Even Simon had noticed. 'What happened to you?' he whined when she yelled at him for not flushing the toilet. 'You never used to mind.'

'I always minded, Simon. Believe me.'

Personally, Pam was glad it was all over and done with. After a certain age (this age) there was something undignified about sex. She could count the lovers in her life on the fingers of one hand. One of her many regrets was not having made it to the second hand. Since her husband Alistair left five years ago she had tried to have other relationships, but even men who had at first appeared reliably stolid eventually turned out to be pillocks. Judge ye them not by their beards. Torquil, for example, the last man she'd had intercourse with (*that wanker you shagged on holiday*, as Simon put it, when he had overheard her talking about it with Fiona W.), had seemed like a completely decent sort and yet his sexual manners and mores had turned out to be considerably less than satisfactory. Torquil was a teacher. It sounded like an alphabet primer. T is for Torquil, Torquil is a teacher. P is for Pam, Pam is ... what *was* Pam, Pam wondered? Prudent, precise, patient? *Pissed off*, Simon would have said more truthfully.

And she'd always been such an optimist! Even in the face of blatant hopelessness (Simon, for example).

She met Torquil at an evening class, An Introduction to Italian Art, a ten-week course which culminated in a three-day trip to Florence. Until their departure for Italy, their intimacy had been restricted to a joint responsibility for coffee and biscuits during the break in class. Torquil made her a badge that said 'Biscuit Monitor', which she had gone to great lengths to avoid wearing ('Oh, no – I left it at home *again*!). It seemed an immature gesture from such a patently mature man. ('Marking my time to retirement'.) Pam had felt no sexual attraction to him at all – this was a man who wore his tie like a noose and possessed a badge machine, for heaven's sake; yet on their first night in Florence, under the influence of a carafe of Chianti and an Italian moon, she led him into her (cramped) hotel room and was surprised to hear herself murmur, 'Let's be reckless tonight.'

'Goodness, Pam,' he said, disrobing himself of his old-fashioned short-sleeved shirt and hanging his trousers carefully over the back of a chair. 'This is a surprise.'

Afterwards, he left her bed for his own, claiming that something in Pam's room was 'bringing on my allergies'. The next morning at breakfast (a disappointingly dull continental affair) he didn't sit at her table even though there was an empty chair right next to hers and when she laughingly accosted him later in the Duomo ('You're not avoiding me, are you?'), he muttered a feeble excuse and sloped off towards some ridiculously over-ornate side-chapel. Pam experienced a sudden aversion to Italian art, prancing and preening like the Whore of Babylon. Give me Protestant gloom any day, Pam thought. She had been brought up without religion: her father was a kind of pagan and her mother was a lapsed daughter of the Free Presbyterian Church. The older Pam grew, the more she lamented not having something unbelievable to fall back on as a comfort in the long, dark hours of her solitary nights.

The members of the book group perked up like meercats at the sound of the front door opening and then crashing shut, closely followed by Simon slamming into the room as if he was pretending to be in the SAS. He flinched at the unexpected sight of a room full of middle-aged women (*old bags*). He couldn't have looked more horrified if he'd stumbled on a coven of naked witches sacrificing a goat on the fitted Axminster. Simon was twenty-one but still showed no sign of growing up.

'Book group,' Pam said to him, helpfully. It would have been nice if he could have managed even a rudimentary 'Hi', shown at least a pretence at manners, but he backed out of the room mumbling something that didn't even try to be a sentence, trailing the intrusive scent of beer and cigarettes in his wake.

The room was silent for a moment as everyone tried to think of something positive to say about Simon. Pam had to resist the desire to fill the void with excuses. ('I did my best' might be top of her list.) Everyone else's offspring were doing interesting post-grads ('International Law with Portuguese') or work placements on magazines in London ('*The Bride* – what fun!'), whereas Simon had been lured into becoming a drone in the headquarters of a big insurance firm that was based in the capital. It ran some kind of graduate entry scheme that fed off boys like Simon. 'They have an ice-cream machine,' he said, when she asked (*interrogated*) him about why he wanted to work there. Now every morning he donned his cheap, chain-store suit in order to sit at a computer all day long, doing something called 'data entry'. What kind of data, Pam wondered? (*Stuff.*) Every evening he crawled reluctantly home via a corporate watering-hole where he supped and sniggered with a group of his co-*frères* (*the guys from the office*). And no thank you, he didn't want to do something 'more creative and fulfilling'. Alarmingly, he actually seemed to like the job.

'He hasn't really found out what he wants to do yet,' Pam said, trying not to sound apologetic.

'Oh, I know,' Charlotte said, all earnest understanding. 'Harry's taken a gap year, helping to build a school in Botswana. But I'm sure he'll settle down to his MPhil when he comes back.'

The information was met with a murmur of approval. 'Good for Harry,' Fiona W. said.

Jolly, jolly good, Pam thought, and had to put her hand over her mouth to stop her sarcasm flying out into the room.

Alistair was irritatingly indifferent to Simon's prospects. 'I don't know why you're complaining,' he said to her, 'you should be glad he's working. God, Pamela, let's be honest, neither of us ever imagined Simon with a *job*.' When had Alistair started calling her 'Pamela' instead of 'Pam'? (And why?) It seemed a shame that Simon didn't have at least one parent who had harboured expectations for him, however small.

Of course, they had just been a practice family as far as Alistair was concerned. Now he was with 'Jenny' (fifteen years younger than Pam, flesh as firm as unripe apricots) and had another two children ('Mimi' and 'Noah'), reprising his first marriage, doing it all over again but better this time. His new, replacement children had a better father in Alistair than Simon or Rebecca ever had. Why had she and Alistair given them such Jewish-sounding names? Pam had always thought she would like to be Jewish; she imagined herself baking a lot in a warm kitchen and being nicer to her children.

'Of course, Rebecca's such a high-flyer,' Fiona W. said, as if Rebecca's talents made up for Simon's deficiencies. Rebecca had recently qualified as a doctor. Pam worried more about Rebecca than she did about Simon. Simon may be lacking in all social niceties but at least he had feelings. Rebecca, on the other hand, was no longer in possession of her soul. Pam suspected her daughter of having traded it the Christmas she was seven, in exchange for My Little Pony's 'Brush Me Beautiful

Boutique', an unlovely item that Pam kept in the attic so that one day in the future she could expose Rebecca's tasteless childhood to her own demon offspring. (*Christ, Mother, don't worry, I'm never having children, I would rather die.*)

'Chalk and cheese, your Simon and Rebecca,' Charlotte laughed. Pam sighed. So many clichés, so little time.

'Still, it must be nice having one of them still living at home,' Fiona G. said, wreathing herself in a pashmina, as the members of the book group trooped into the hallway and started struggling into layers of outdoor clothes.

'Well ...' Pam said, as the smell of something illegal drifted down the stairs, 'in some respects.'

'They never leave any more, do they?' Honor said cheerfully. 'Goodness knows, I couldn't wait to leave home. I don't know what's wrong with them. I can't remember – did we agree on the Tony Parsons for next time?'

Once they had all left, Pam ran a bath and lay in it imagining what it would be like to be in her coffin. Perhaps they wouldn't bury her. Rebecca was more likely to choose cremation and it seemed unlikely that Simon would have any opinion in the matter. Perhaps she should make a preference clear to them now. Did she have a preference? Burn or rot? Which would be better?

She tried to put tomorrow's lesson plans together in her mind. She had returned to teaching recently after a disastrous foray into the world of business (handmade wedding favours – how many marriages had been blighted by her misshapen tartan bows and baskets of foil-wrapped chocolate hearts?). She was good at teaching, it was just a shame that children were so bad at being taught. Her higher class were doing Donne's *Holy Sonnets.* 'I am a little world made cunningly/Of elements, and an angelic sprite.' They didn't understand a word, of course.

It was extraordinary how huge her belly looked in the bath, a great white mound of cottage cheese or a shapeless blancmange. She'd plumped up a lot recently, like a cushion, like a turkey. Was she really this fat? (*Christ, Mother, you're like a heifer. You're really letting yourself go.*) The blancmange belly wasn't as soft as it looked. Something fluttered inside, a small trapped bird making a bid for flight. Perhaps she had a tumour. She imagined a tumour growing inside her, pushing other organs bullishly aside, like an assertive baby. That, at least, was impossible, thank God. Sex with Torquil the Teacher had taken place well over a year ago and now she had arrived in the barren lands.

Squinting down at her body through the miasma of steam rising from the bath, she thought she could make out her belly rippling and erupting like a mud pool. Gas, probably, another unfortunate effect of aging. It looked as if something small and ferocious was trying to punch its way out. She felt suddenly squeamish.

'Jesus Christ, Mum,' Simon yelled at her aggressively from the other side of the bathroom door. 'How long are you going to be in there? I need a crap.'

'Thank you for sharing that, Simon.' If she had realised he was going to move back home she would have put in a second bathroom.

A foot. That was definitely a foot. What in God's name? She gave a little cry and heaved herself abruptly out of the bath, dripping water like a great mythic sea creature rising from the deep.

'Mum? Mum, what are you *doing* in there?'

Immaculate conception. The Annunciation happening at a moment when she'd been distracted, sometime last September probably, round about the traumatic time of the school inspection. There'd been a lot of stress at school, enough to take your mind off the Holy Ghost breathing into your ear, or whatever it was that a patriarchal religion did to avoid the horror of intimacy with a woman's sexual organs (or indeed the woman they were attached to). Gabriel murmuring the Word of God, sending it to the womb via the heart instead of the vagina. Pam had looked up a lot of this stuff online. Some of it was quite alarming.

And in the Convent of San Marco in Florence, hadn't there been a Filippo Lippi painting of the

Annunciation where a dove was caught in the act of flying into the Virgin's ear? What happened when it arrived? Did it enter the ear (distressing for both Virgin and dove, she imagined) or did it perch on the lobe and whisper sweet nothings to the Chosen One?

Or, Pam wondered, had a different god appeared to her, perhaps disguised as an eagle, a bull, a shower of gold? Or a swan. Plenty of swans on Blackford Pond – she frequently fed bread to them. Perhaps one had snuck up on her when she was preoccupied with Simon's incipient drug habit or Rebecca's missing soul. Should she consider herself lucky that she had given birth to a baby rather than laying an egg? (Although that would have been less messy.) What about alien abduction? Should she consider that? Which was more likely – divine or alien impregnation? Both seemed equally improbable. It wasn't as if she could ask anyone: she would find herself on a psychiatric ward in a heartbeat. Simon believed in aliens but that in itself was evidence of his unsuitability to counsel her. Pam wondered if she should start going to church. Bit late now perhaps.

She hadn't told Rebecca. She couldn't bear how disgusted she would be at the idea of a sibling (*Christ, Mother, at your age?*). Actually she hadn't told anyone she knew, apart from Simon (although not the immaculate conception part) and only because it was unavoidable. Even Simon, as self-obsessed as he was, would have eventually noticed the presence of a baby in the house.

The baby showed no sign of having either alien or holy blood in its veins. It looked like every other baby, thank goodness. *A little world made cunningly.* There were no rules, or at least none that Pam had managed to discover, that dictated the second time around should be a replica of the first. Virgin births, midwinter, wise men, shepherds, mangers, not to mention all the trappings of an agrarian Judaic culture – none of these were necessarily relevant. Why shouldn't the Second Coming be ushered in by a middle-aged, dispirited divorcee in the maternity ward of the Royal Infirmary, at the fag end of Western civilisation? Stranger things had happened. On second thoughts, perhaps they hadn't.

Thank God it was easy. 'You've done this before,' the midwife laughed.

'In some respects,' Pam said.

Pam had forgotten how much she liked babies. Each one a possibility, each one a fresh start, a hope and a wish for the world.

Names were a problem. What on earth do you call the saviour of the world – Demi, Ashley, Jade? (Mimi? Hardly.) She had another week before she had to register the birth. She wondered about 'Grace' – abstract yet symbolic.

She didn't hear the baby crying at first. She *did* cry (it was a baby, after all), although not excessively, doing everything with a kind of Buddhist-like moderation. By the time Pam had made her way up the stairs, the baby had reduced her crying to no more than an untroubled whimper, calmed by an unseen hand. Someone was in the nursery. Pam's heart started pounding as she ran up the last few steps.

She stopped on the threshold, astonished by the sight before her. Simon was cradling the baby, holding its cocoon-body against his shoulder while he waltzed ineptly around the room. He was humming something (he was the most unmusical of boys) and it took Pam a few seconds to recognise the tune as a lullaby. She wondered if he'd been taking drugs. He caught sight of her and said, 'I think she had wind.' He handed the bundle of sleeping baby over to Pam. Pam wondered if she had witnessed the baby's first small miracle. Simon gave her an embarrassed smile and shrugged before loping out of the room, not without tripping over the carpet and banging his elbow on the door-jamb. Pam wondered how he had managed to survive intact for twenty-one years.

She held the unlooked-for gift of the baby in her arms, felt its soft weight and kissed the silk floss on the fragile shell of its head. How on earth was she going to manage? But if not her, then who?

'My mum taught me my love of books, of words and of good music.

Thanks to her I could read before I went to school and I grew up to the soundtrack of Dusty Springfield, the Rolling Stones, the Animals and Bob Dylan.

To this day she writes me hilariously funny letters, especially when she is away on holiday. I don't get postcards, I get travelogues!

There wasn't much money around when I was really young.

My mum and dad were still in their teens and I know now that things were tough for them financially, but all I can remember is lots of fun and a real sense of security.

No one has a bad word to say
about my mum.

She's funny, kind, good and wise.'

Lorraine Kelly

The Reluctant Mother

Lisa Jewell

It's early – very early. I'm hung over. I pour myself a large glass of water and peer groggily through the kitchen window. It is drizzling and the sky is granite grey and barely lit. A man emerges from a flat over the road. He is fully dressed and has a small baby tucked under his arm. With the other arm he unlocks the boot of his car, pulls out a folded pushchair and erects it. He then puts the baby into the pushchair, fiddles around with the straps, pulls a plastic hood over the pram and heads off down the road. He looks, bizarrely, quite content. He is almost jaunty. I shudder and head back to bed where I will stay for at least another four hours, possibly longer. I am thirty. I have no children. I am glad.

I am standing in a friend's garden. It is late evening and the sun is setting beyond the rooftops. My friend has twelve cats, all of whom have arranged themselves into graceful silhouettes along the garden fence. I realise that all the grown-ups have gone inside, that I am alone in the garden with my friend's daughter whom I have only just met. I feel awkward, as if I should say something. 'Which one's your favourite?' I open, genially. She glances at me, seven-year-old eyes slanted with disdain. 'I don't *have* a favourite,' she hisses. Then she turns, slowly, and heads indoors. I am alone. And I am, to my great horror, crying. Yes, crying – because a seven-year-old girl wasn't very nice to me. I am thirty-one years old. I have no children. I am relieved.

I am in the beer garden of our local pub. A baby is crying in my friend's arms. It is her baby. She gave birth to it two months ago, and all it does is cry. Another friend arrives with her partner and their baby. I don't notice the baby at first. It is two weeks old and nestled inside a thick cotton strap around her torso. Half of us have children. Half of us don't. My friends with children sip mineral water and pace back and forth, fretting and placating. After about half an hour they go. The child-free are left alone. I pick up my full pint of lager and feel smug. I am thirty-two years old. I have no children. I am delighted.

We're sitting outside a café, just off Oxford Street, me, my mother, my sisters. We've had lunch together and bought clothes together and now we're having a nice cup of tea. I don't know where it comes from, the question, but it spills from my mouth, suddenly and dramatically, between sips of Earl Grey.

'What's the payback?'

My sister realises I'm addressing her, stares at me blankly. 'What do you mean?'

'I mean, children. Where's the payback? What do you get out of it?'

She continues to stare at me blankly. 'I don't understand.' Her face is a picture of genuine, uncomprehending confusion. My mother understands the question and steps into the void. 'This,' she says, gesturing at her three girls, 'this is what it's all about.'

I nod, satisfied. That is a concept I can relate to. While I hate the idea of 'children', I love the idea of 'family'. I want my very own adults; big, handsome sons; beautiful, headstrong daughters.

'No,' says my sister. She looks slightly appalled. 'That's not it. That's not the best bit.'

'You mean you're not looking forward to your children growing up?'

'Of course not. I want my children to live with me for ever. I don't ever want them to grow up.'

Now I am confused. Why would a strong-minded, intelligent, beautiful woman want to be saddled with kids for ever? Why is she not desperate for them to go so that she can get on with her life again, unencumbered, free?

'When you have children,' she continues, 'it's the

best thing in the whole world. You just want them to be children for ever. It's like magic.'

I think of her son, my nephew. He is clever, funny, energetic, delightful, manic, infuriating, loving, trying, disobedient, exhausting. I look forward to seeing him, and then, when it is time to go, I look forward to getting into my car, alone, without anyone dragging me out into the garden to play with gravel, without anyone bombarding me with questions, without anyone following me into the toilet.

I sigh. I am thirty-three years old. And I'm still no closer to understanding what on earth children are for.

I never wanted children. As a teenager I had it all planned. I'd stay single until I was forty and then I'd marry a divorcé who already had children. That way I would get all the benefits of adult children – weddings, grandchildren, people to have Sunday lunch with – without actually having to go through the ignominy, pain and bother of having a child of my own .

I don't know where this stridently non-maternal streak came from. Well, maybe I do. My mother couldn't wait for my sisters and me to leave home. She left us in no doubt that once she'd emptied her home of children, she'd be able to get on with her life again. My middle sister left first, at sixteen, I left next at seventeen. My youngest sister left when she was eighteen. Despite our mother's naked desire for us all to go at the earliest possible opportunity, she was a very good mother. She was there. She was present. We never felt insecure or unloved. She just felt that mothering was a finite job, a project with a beginning, a middle and an end. She could see another life for herself on the other side of mothering and she liked the look of it, that was all. And maybe that's why I didn't think I wanted children – maybe I could see her point.

But at the age of thirty-one, I blew my teenage master plan by marrying a man who had no children of his own. I dealt with the fact that I was no nearer wanting children as a married woman of thirty-one than I had been as a teenager by telling myself, and all and sundry, that I would start a family when I was forty. That seemed reasonable enough and tucked away somewhere, in the far distant future. In the meantime I got on with the glorious, liberated, self-centred business of being myself.

I am thirty-three and a half. Nearly everyone I know has become a parent and I'm pretty sure there's a conspiracy going on. I secretly believe that they all hate being parents and that they spout all this 'magic' hogwash because they can't admit the truth – that they've made a terrible, dreadful mistake, that their lives are ruined. When friends try to persuade me to have children I think they're jealous of my freedom and want me to be as unhappy as them. I don't believe the clichés – oh, it's different when they're your own. How can it be different? A kid is a kid is a kid. What does it matter where it came from?

But then something strange happens to me. I feel vague flutterings of broodiness. They are slight, barely perceptible in fact, but I pounce on them eagerly. I always assumed I'd have to force myself to want a baby but now, suddenly, my body is sending me tiny little radar beeps to let me know that it is maybe, just possibly, ready to consider it. It isn't what you might call baby hunger, but it's better than nothing.

We start trying on 1st January 2002. After using contraception for the best part of fifteen years, it comes as something of a surprise when I don't fall pregnant at the merest hint of unfettered sperm, but I breathe a sigh of relief when my period arrives a couple of weeks later. I feel a sense of reprieve. I can keep drinking, keep smoking, keep on being 'me' for a few weeks more. We try for ten months and the longer we try, the more ambivalent I become. I don't really care if there's something wrong with me or something wrong with my husband. If we can't have babies then fine, we'll have lots of holidays and lots of fun and lots of nice meals instead.

It is ten months into Project Baby and I am reading *A Life's Work* by Rachel Cusk. I turn the pages, feverishly, numbly, in horror. This is the author's account of her first year of motherhood and it is reinforcing every single misgiving and dread I've had about motherhood. Yes, says Rachel, you will lose your identity. Yes, you will feel isolated and cut off from everything. Yes, your old life will fade away like some distant, glorious, long-forgotten dream. Yes, your husband will disappear every morning, into what used to be your world, and leave you at home, resentful and scared with a weird little baby to look after. Yes, babies are a nightmare, they cry and cry and cry, and then they cry some more. Yes, says Rachel Cusk, motherhood is hell.

'Jascha,' I say, 'I'm not sure about this. I'm not sure I'm ready. Can we stop trying for a while?'

So we do. We stop trying. We avoid my fertile period as assiduously as we targeted it for the preceding ten months. I feel relieved and free. My body is my own again. My life is my own. No demanding, draining, identity-snatching baby is going to be allowed to come along and mess everything up. But then, two days before my period is due, I have a funny feeling. It's highly unlikely that I'm pregnant but it suddenly occurs to me that I might be. So I unpeel the last of my pregnancy testers and I take it into the toilet with me.

And lo and behold, there it is, a white plastic stick with two pink lines on it. I phone my sister. I phone my mother. I phone my other sister. I pace the flat, wondering how I feel about this miracle conception, about the fact of my impending motherhood. Jascha comes home that night with a bunch of pink roses and an uncertain smile. Later on, we sit in a wine bar and I have a glass of champagne. I sip it gingerly, feeling strangely unfazed by my inability to drink whatever I want. I feel sanguine. Not excited, not thrilled, just *sanguine*.

When I fail to start throwing up or develop weird cravings or feel tearful or tired or tetchy, I decide that I can't possibly be pregnant. I spend about £30 on pregnancy tests over the course of the next three weeks. They all show positive but still I don't believe them, so I spend another £175 to have an early scan. And there it is, a tiny blob clinging to the lining of my womb and a loud, thumping, insistent heartbeat reverberating around the consulting room.

I take the shiny sliver of paper home and show the formless blob to Jascha. Finally, I feel pregnant. And I love it. I really love it. I love all the fuss and the attention. I love being so conspicuous, like a ship in full sail. I love being sober at parties, being this huge, slow-moving but totally independent creature, easing myself in and out of my sports car, meeting friends for lunch in town. I wear my pregnancy like a beautiful new dress, accepting compliments for it wherever I go.

But I am still in denial about what is about to happen to me. As far as I am concerned, I am pregnant but there *is not* going to be a baby. I avoid prams in the street like you might avoid a drunk tramp. In the changing rooms at my gym, I sweep through the mayhem of the 'family' area, through the buggies and shouting mothers, the piles of wet towels and cartoons blaring from the television, towards the door that says 'Children are not permitted to play in this area'. I fear for the day when I will not be allowed to come in here any more. My mother buys the baby some trousers in soft white jersey and a vest with a small animal embroidered on the breast. I keep them in the spare room and visit them every now and then. Sometimes I look at them and have to leave the room immediately; other times I pick them up and stare at them in nervous disbelief. How can it be possible that I am going to produce something from my body that will one day inhabit these tiny bits of cotton? How can it be possible that there is going to be a baby living in our house?

We go to see our friend's new baby two weeks before ours is due. I watch Georgia on the sofa, guiding her gigantic nipples into the mouth of her new baby. I quake. In the car on the way home I start to cry. I don't want that to be me. I don't want a deflated stomach and that slightly manic look of bliss in my eyes and a child attached to my breasts. I want to keep her in my tummy where she can look after herself. I don't want to be a mother. I just want to be pregnant. I am thirty-five years old. I am eight and a half months pregnant. I still don't want a child.

At my last scan my consultant tells me that my little girl is breech. Unless she turns in the next fourteen days I will have to have a Caesarean. She doesn't turn, despite the best efforts of a well-meaning acupuncturist with a handful of needles and a couple of sticks of incense.

So now I have a date.

I could put it in my diary if I liked: *29th July 9am – Have baby.*

On 28th July I get the bus into town and do my last ever walk of freedom. I haul my vast body down Oxford Street, I buy myself a necklace, I eat alone at the sushi conveyor belt in Selfridges. I feel melancholic. This, I tell myself, is the end of 'me'. Jascha and I go out for our last meal that night as a childless couple. We end the pregnancy, as we'd begun it, sipping champagne in our local wine bar. And then we go home.

It's the strangest feeling, going to bed that night, knowing that tomorrow morning everything in my world is about to spin round 360° on its axis and come crashing down somewhere new and terrifying. I don't expect to sleep, but I do.

The next morning is warm and bright. Jascha's parents drive us to the hospital. A midwife comes to give me a final palpation. As her hands press into the taut skin of my belly, she grimaces. Hmm, she says, I think she might have turned. I feel a sunray of hope. If she's turned then I won't have to have a Caesarean. If she's turned, I can go home and not be a mother! The consultant is called and I am given an ultrasound scan. The midwife was wrong. My baby girl is standing proud, straight as a soldier. Motherhood is moments away.

We are taken down to surgery where I am stripped and redressed in a cotton smock and Jascha is given a suit of green scrubs. I am administered a drip and an epidural, and then a curtain is dropped between me and the lower half of my body. Jascha peers over halfway through the procedure and still talks about what he saw to this day: 'Your actual intestines!' I feel my flesh being pulled and tugged and pulled again, and then I see her.

She is a round-faced, yellow-haired angel with a wide, screaming mouth.

'Oh my God, oh God, Jascha, did you see her? Did you see her? Oh my God, she's so beautiful, so beautiful.' I am gabbling and gushing, stupefied with pride and joy. She is wrapped in white towelling and brought back to me, her fully made-up mother in a paper hat. I am living the cliché, the moment of utter perfection, the waves of intense and instantaneous love. She is everything I could have hoped for and more. The prettiest, best baby that anyone has ever given birth to. The centre of everything. The greatest achievement of my life.

We are wheeled into the recovery room and a midwife appears by my side, clutching my new baby. 'Right,' she says, 'are you ready to try for your first feed?'

Perhaps unsurprisingly, my attitude towards breastfeeding has always been somewhat negative. I find it very hard to separate the process from the sexuality of the organs. I don't like seeing women breastfeeding in public. What they're doing, in my opinion, is comparable to going to the loo and they should go and sit in a toilet cubicle and do it there, where I can't see them. When my own friends breastfeed their children in front of me I feel uncomfortable. If they breastfeed their children beyond the newborn stage I start to question their motives. Why are they still breastfeeding their babies? Are they getting some kind of sick kick out of it?

My sisters and I were not breastfed by our mother. Our lips never so much as glanced against her nipples. My younger sister breastfed her son for the first two weeks, specifically to give him her colostrum, and then she stopped, claiming that it was every bit as horrible as she'd expected it would be. So I assumed that I would want to take the same approach; a couple of weeks of awkward, unpleasant breastfeeding, for the sake of the baby, and then I would reclaim my breasts and hand my husband a hungry baby and a nice warm bottle of SMA.

But I have no such feelings of doubt or ambivalence as the midwife hands me my brand new baby this morning. I am ready to do anything, absolutely anything for this little parcel of fleshy perfection. She is laid across my chest and she pulls my nipple into her mouth and I wait, ready for failure, ready for pain, ready for something to go wrong. Everything I've read, while pregnant, about breastfeeding has been negative (or maybe I only absorbed the negative stuff as the positive stuff made me feel weird), but there is no discomfort and there is no failure. She sucks and she sucks and she sucks. She sucks non-stop for the first half an hour of her life and gets a full belly of milk. 'I can't believe how well she's doing,' I say to the midwife.

'That's probably because you've got such well-shaped nipples,' she says, smiling.

This is the greatest compliment I have ever been paid in my life.

So here I am. Thirty-five years old and a mother, in spite of possessing no maternal instincts, in spite of years of ambivalence, in spite of weird children making me cry and in spite of Rachel Cusk.

I wait and wait for everything to feel different, but it doesn't happen. True, I spend my time differently, but inside my head, inside my heart, I am still, fundamentally, exactly the same. My baby, I soon realise, is not an appendage but an extension of myself. So not only do I still feel like 'me', but I feel even *more* sure of myself and who I am.

I am Lisa Jewell, wife, daughter, sister, friend, successful author and *mother*. I feel empowered and fulfilled by my new role in life. And Amelie, of course, is remarkable. I keep her close to me at all times. My mother comes to see us one evening. As I open the door to her she says, 'You know, you haven't come to the door to me once without that baby in your arms.'

My mother is always trying to get me to put her down, but Amelie doesn't want to be put down and I don't particularly want to put her down. I use a sling instead of a pram, loving the feeling of her body next to mine, wanting her to see the world from my perspective. I use a sling, in fact, until she is eleven months old, until the insteps of my feet have nearly collapsed under the strain. And of course I breastfeed her for as long as she wants to be breastfed, until she gets bored of disappearing under my top every morning and wants to do other things instead.

Oh my goodness, I am this close to becoming an earth mother.

Amelie is two and a half now. She's superb. In fact, she's so superb that for a long time I didn't think I'd want another baby, in case it wasn't as good as her. I went off babies again, completely, wanted nothing to do with them. When I looked back on the first demanding months of Amelie's life I was amazed not only that I got through it, but that I actually *enjoyed* it.

Babies are so *boring* compared to toddlers. They're little and silly and unpredictable, and they wake up in the middle of the night. Why would I put myself through that all over again?

But then, late last year, I heard a familiar radar beep coming from somewhere deep inside me and realised that it was time, time to make another baby. We've been trying for three months, but this time there's no ambivalence. This time I want a baby so much I ache. This time I feel green with envy every time I see a pregnant woman. This time I peer into prams instead of avoiding them. I've just bought myself a Persona ovulation predictor. It cost £50. I don't want to leave it to chance.

All the clichés are true. Children do enhance your life. There is no conspiracy. Everyone was telling the truth. And the only reason why people who have had children are so desperate for you to join them on the other side is because they know how much you're going to love it. If I hadn't had a baby, I wouldn't know any of this and I'm sure I'd have been every bit as happy as I am now. I have a great relationship, a great family, great friends and a great career. My life would have been fulfilling and satisfying without a child in it. But I'm thrilled I've got one, and amazed by how little has really changed. Children, you see, enjoy nice holidays in exotic countries and meals in smart restaurants just as much as you do. And most good restaurants open at six o'clock. Children like going on tubes and like going for walks and like seeing friends for lunch. My child even likes sitting in the back seat of my car listening to Xfm. We sing along to the Arctic Monkeys and she tells me off if I turn the volume down. 'Make it loud!' she says, 'make it loud!'

For every bad afternoon there are ten superb afternoons. For every tantrum there is a cuddle. For every sick stain on your carpet there is a stranger's smile on the street. And for every broken night there is a walk through the park on a sunny day, when the sunlight catches the soft wisps of your child's hair and they turn and smile at you in wonder at their first sighting of a squirrel; and they're dressed in a coat that gave you just as much pleasure to buy as a £200 jacket from Whistles, and as far as you're concerned they are the most beautiful, enchanting, wondrous and special child ever to have been brought into existence. And you are the luckiest woman in the world.

I'll look after the baby. Why don't you just relax and make dinner?

Oh, Lovely Ones

Isla Dewar

I think my mother must have been a groupie. She loved the Wild West Show, and went with one or other of her six sisters once a week when it was playing. It must have been quite a spectacle – Indians, cowboys, Mexicans, buffalo and wild horses. There were depictions of battles and Indian villages. My mother, Agnes Ellis Pierce, must have been thrilled.

She was probably even more thrilled when she caught the eye of one of the cast, an actual North American Indian. She was a striking woman, I'm told, tall, with a mane of chestnut hair that she wore in a bun. The affair couldn't have lasted long, the show played from November 1891 to February the following year. He sailed back to his homeland leaving her with his sacred Ghost Shirt and me.

I like to think of my mother and father in that big box bed in the flat where she, a widow with six children, lived in the Byres Road. I imagine her letting her hair fall down past her breasts, and him, huge and tender, stroking it, singing Lakota love songs and lullabies to her. Perhaps it wasn't like that at all. Perhaps she lay with him in the quarters he slept in with the show. I don't know. Whatever, after he left she never saw or heard from him again. Back then, it must have been quite a scandal.

One thing I do know, I am the seventh daughter of a seventh daughter, my father was the seventh son of a seventh son, I believe this goes some way to explain my condition, which is not painful, just brutal, and, by now, more than a little wearing; a curse that, in fact, until recently, went on and on.

When he left to sail home to America, my father stroked my mother's pregnant belly and told her to call me Constant Water. That's me, Emily Constant Water Pierce. All my children are called Water – Silent Water, Shining Water, Still Water. Oh, there're too many to mention here. I have a little tribe of my own, and all of them female.

Eighteen-ninety, what a year that must have been for my father. I'm fairly sure he must have been one of Kicking Bear's companions when he travelled, with the great Sitting Bull's permission, to visit Wovoka, the Paiute mystic, and, some say, messiah. It was a journey that would take him from the Dakota territories to Nevada and on to Glasgow.

Wovoka foretold an apocalypse – thousands of tons of earth would fall from the sky, burying all white men. Following this deluge, grass would grow lush and green, sweet rivers of water would flow and wild horses, antelope and buffalo would return to the plains. You can see the appeal of this to people herded into reservations where the land was so poor nothing grew. They were starving.

The Indians would be raised into the air when this avalanche of earth fell, heralding a new spring, but only those who believed in the Ghost Dance religion. This involved ritual cleansing, prayers, meditation and performing the actual ghost dance – a sort of anticlockwise shuffle that went on for hours, days even. There was chanting. There was frenzy. Ghost dancers were known to fall into a coma, die even. And the hysteria it caused scared the pants off the white settlers. They thought it would lead to violence. It was banned. My father, I know, continued to perform it. It was those Lakota Indians who followed the Ghost Dance religion, who were massacred at Wounded Knee. My father was not there, but he must have lost relatives and friends. He was arrested in one of the skirmishes that followed the massacre and told he could either serve life imprisonment in Fort Sheridan or join the Wild West Show. Not a lot of choice there, then. I'd have joined Buffalo Bill, too.

The show's depiction of the Battle of Little Big Horn showed the Sioux as sneaky, greasy savages who ambushed the great General Custer: not true. It must have been heartbreaking for the Indians to go through this ritual. It was their punishment. It was also thought that a glimpse of the great European cities would put the savage renegades in awe of the mighty White Man.

I'm thinking it must have been a very angry man who fetched up in Glasgow, in November 1891. What did he make of it? I imagine him, in full regalia, standing in Sauchiehall Street, looking around, hemmed in by buildings and stared at by passers-by. And what did he make of the small flat off Byers Road where my mother lived with her six children? Did he find comfort in her bed? Or was it too soft for him? My older sister, Etta, remembered him. 'He was huge,' she said. 'Filled the room. But he never stayed long.' She thought he found the three-roomed flat claustrophobic. 'He'd pace,' she said. 'He liked to keep the windows open, though it was freezing outside.' Apparently he was fond of a dram.

I have my father's Ghost Shirt. It is decorated with magical symbols, meant to shield its wearer from the white man's bullets. It didn't work, obviously. I keep it wrapped in tissue in the chest of drawers in my bedroom. I have worn it. I have put it on in times of stress and shuffled anticlockwise, chanting. I do this at night when the curtains are drawn, and as quietly as I can. I don't know what the neighbours would make of it. I can tell you this – the Ghost Shirt is equally ineffectual against heartache, loneliness, demands from the Inland Revenue and parking wardens. It is a beautiful and useless thing.

Actually, I visited the Lakota tribe, or what remained of them in Dakota, in 1954. I stayed in Rapid City and travelled about in a rented car visiting the Cheyenne River, Crow Creek, Bear Butte – oh, all sorts of places. I wanted only to see, to smell, to breathe the air of the country of my ancestors.

I met Bessie May Blue Shield in a diner not far outside Pierre. It was hot; I'd gone in for something cold to drink. A Coke. I try not to drink alcohol. She had a face older than time, cracked as dry leather, but her eyes were clear and brown. She hadn't many teeth. Her ancient body was thin, frail, looked so aged it might just crumble beneath your hand if you touched it. She was wearing a bowler hat with a feather in the band. I thought she looked fine. 'You are One,' she said.

'One what?'

'One.'

I shrugged. But I had a feeling I knew what she was talking about. I was sixty-three and looked about twenty-five.

'You can see ahead,' she said.

Indeed I can, I have the second sight. I often wish I hadn't.

'You will have many many more children,' said Bessie May.

'No I won't. I've had eight. I'm done with all that.'

She laughed and told me I was One. A mother of mothers and there would be more daughters to come. 'And they will keep you young. But beware of the golden.' I didn't know what that meant.

'The golden one will steal your heart, make you laugh. But, if you have his boy child, you will no longer be One.'

'Then what?' I asked.

'Then you will look like a mother of too many daughters.' She took off her hat, revealing a balding head sparsely covered with thin white hair. She waved her hands over her bent, crumbling body, her toothless, cracked, wizened face. 'You will look like me.'

My blood chilled. Who would want to look like that? I figured all I had to do was avoid men with golden hair, gold jewellery, gold-coloured shoes, clothes, everything golden in fact, and all would be fine.

As for never having a boy child, I have no problem with that. I like having daughters. This time we are living through, this century, is a time for women. I'm proud of my girls.

Despite my colourful ancestry, I have led a mundane life. My mother died not long after I was born. She aged suddenly and dramatically. Seemed to crumble away, I'm told. I was brought up in that same flat where my father paced and swigged whisky and dreamed of his homeland, according to my sister Etta. She married Tam, a draper by trade, and they had four children. I helped to look after them. I loved their little faces and boisterous games. Etta said I had a way with bairns. 'You're born to be a mother.' She was right. Here I am with nineteen daughters, well, twenty if you count my little Eleanor, thirty-six granddaughters and ten great-granddaughters – a mother of mothers.

And it isn't easy. Christmas is hell. So many presents, so many cards, so much bickering about who I'm going to this year. Obviously, they can't all come to me. I don't have the chairs, the plates, the spoons. There isn't a turkey in the world big enough. But we manage. There is a lot of love.

My first love was John Duffy. Oh, he was a lovely man – long lashes, brown and soulful eyes and gentle hands. He was a clerk in a shipping office. We married in 1914; I was twenty-two. He said I looked like a little squaw with my dark eyes and dark hair and high cheekbones. He was never unkind about my nose, which is a little hooked and too large for modern tastes. And he didn't mind that I was a fatherless child, born out of wedlock – which was a terrible thing back then.

When he went away, he kissed my eyes, 'Goodbye

eyes.' Then my lips, 'Goodbye lips.' And so tender was it all, I can still, if I try, feel his touch on my face. He died at Ypres. And I took to wearing the black.

My little Eleanor Hushed Water was born three months after I got that awful telegram. She was a beautiful little thing, brown eyes and long lashes like her father. The diphtheria took her when she was two. And I took to wearing the black again. I wore it for four years. I walked slowly. I looked at the ground wherever I went. I grieved. I worked six days a week in my sister's husband's draper's shop, and went to the kirk on Sundays.

That's where I met Henry Campbell. He was a doctor, a widower, and fifteen years older than me. He was looking for someone to serve him supper, to answer his phone, share his bed and give him babies. His last marriage had been childless.

I suppose my sister nagged me into marrying Henry. She said I was facing a life on the shelf. 'A spinster.' She was emphatic about that. 'Nobody else will have you. Face it, this is the last chance of getting yourself a husband. You're old.' I was twenty-six at the time.

He was a dour man, Henry. He liked breakfast on the table at seven thirty every morning, lunch at one and dinner at six. I never failed him. As for babies, I made him the proud father of six wonderful daughters. I loved them all. But it was a hard life, cooking and cleaning and tending to babies, not a lot of time for play. But play we did, singing round the piano (my fourth child, Hannah Joyful Water, had a gift for music), or we'd have a game of hide and seek, running up and down the stairs. Sometimes we sat at the kitchen table with a deck of cards. Henry never joined in. Most evenings, he'd enjoy a glass of port, or two or three or four, in front of the fire, then snooze till bedtime – nine thirty. If it hadn't been for my girls, I'd have died of boredom married to Henry Campbell.

In 1932 we moved to the house in Bearsden, where I still live. Henry had the front two rooms as his surgery. I was receptionist, looking after his patients as they waited to see him, keeping his appointment books, recognising malingerers and those who were seriously ill. It was at this point in my life when I realised I had the second sight. I could tell what was wrong with people before my husband examined them. 'It's George McDuff,' I'd say. 'He has rheumatism.' Or, 'It's Maureen Clark, she's pregnant again. A boy.'

Henry would rage at me. 'How do you know what ails people?' he'd say.

I'd shrug and tell him it was something to do with seeing so many ill people. 'You get a nose for their illnesses.'

'Well, stop telling me what's wrong with my patients. I'm the doctor. I have passed the exams, done the work. You know nothing about medicine.'

I told him I would stop. He was a man of logic. He'd have scorned my gift. Besides, by then, I knew he had only a short time to live. I did tell him to slow down and cut down on the port but he ignored me. He died in 1937, shortly after our sixth daughter, Susan Heavenly Water, was born.

If you are One, it doesn't do to count. I have discovered that. For example, I have lived in my house for seventy-four years. I have washed the windows almost nine hundred times. I have dusted the dresser in the living room over twenty-seven thousand times. I have, I once worked out, changed over eighty-seven thousand nappies. It makes a woman want to lie down in a darkened room.

So many children, grandchildren and now great-grandchildren, little people running through my house and up and down my garden, I wonder what my neighbours make of it. I don't know any of them any more. Time was, everybody knew everybody. Now they are just people who come and go in their shiny cars and nod when I pass them in the street.

I live a life of quiet domesticity, an interior life. I don't go out much these days, just to shop and to the post office with my parcels of potions that I send across the world. I used to be wife, lover and mother. For the past years, I have been only a mother. I cook, I watch them grow, I listen. I have seen those daughters of mine through love affairs, marriages, births, divorces, job losses, career highs and lows, heartache and death. I have offered advice and I have learned when not to offer advice. I know there are moments when all I need to give them is a box of tissues. Then again, there are times when a cheque is needed. They leave home, make their way, lose their way, come home again and leave again. Sometimes I feel that I say too many goodbyes. It pains me.

They visit, they sit at the kitchen table and tell me their lives. Some live in other countries. They phone and send cards and email. I have nursed wounds, both physical and emotional, forked out for longed-for, must-have items, listened to dreadful music, given boyfriends the once-over, cooked favourite meals, sewed on patches and buttons, ironed, nagged, perused homework, sat through school concerts, mashed many thousands of bananas – oh, this list is endless. In this interior life I lead, I think about my girls most of the time. It's almost as if nothing else matters. They are who I am.

The thing that I can't tell them is I know the path their lives will follow. I have the second sight. It is simple for me. It isn't a vision that comes in a dream, or anything I conjure up gazing into a crystal ball. I can see it in their faces. I can see the marks time and experience will leave on them. The changes they will make.

The first time it happened was with my third child, Marie High Water. I was serving supper, bringing a bowl of soup to the table. She turned and said in a whiny sing-song voice, 'Not soup. I hate soup.' And I saw her face change. The young cheeks tightened, the lips became drawn and there was a hardness in her eyes. On that little body, I saw an old, embittered, lonely woman.

The shock of it made me cry out and drop the bowl. It shattered, splattering broth over the floor and over my feet. But I couldn't tell anyone why this had happened. I simply said the bowl had been too hot, and I'd burned my fingers. Poor Marie married too young, went through a nasty divorce, started up a business (a shoe shop), went bankrupt, lost her heart to a hairdresser who left her when her child was two weeks old. Her face when she died at sixty-eight, alone and bitter, was exactly as I'd seen it all those years ago.

This has happened with all my children. It is a moment when their faces shift into what they will become, what love, envy, greed, generosity, music, children – life, in fact – will do to them. Sometimes it brings me joy, sometimes it makes me curl into myself, clutching my belly, filled with grief and trepidation.

I can see into my lovers' faces. Once I looked into the eyes of Eric Reynolds, my seventies man, father of three of my daughters, and saw another woman's eyes look back at me. I knew he was being unfaithful and sent him packing. I saw greed and lust in the face of Richard David, my eighties man, and refused to let him handle my company accounts. In my nineties man, Jeff Morrison, I saw tenderness, openness and honesty. I saw the cancer that would kill him, too. But for him I abandoned my policy of having a bed to myself. We lived together for fourteen years and had one child, Justine Tumbling Water, who is everything her name suggests. She is a child of her times, a handful, demanding, intelligent, wise beyond her years, and I adore her.

The war started two years after Henry died. I worked in the shipyards, not as a welder as I'd liked to have done, but in the offices filing and answering the phones – a dogsbody. But I liked it. I met James Connolly, a fine man. He couldn't join up to fight, something to do with his feet. But he was jolly and I enjoyed his company enough to have two more daughters. We parted when I refused to marry him. I was approaching fifty and getting overly fond of having my bed to myself.

During the war, I turned my whole garden over to growing vegetables and fruit. We ate well enough even if sugar and meat were scarce. But I discovered I had a way with nature. Things in my garden flourished. I grew some herbs – rosemary, thyme and sage. When little Norma Luscious Water developed eczema I made a potion, pounded herbs into a thick cream to soothe the itch. It worked. Not only did her raw and peeling skin heal, it became soft, silky-smooth. It was Luscious who insisted I make more of the cream to sell to neighbours, women whose hands showed the toll of scrubbing and scouring. It didn't take long for my cream to catch on. It was in demand, at sixpence a tub, and I made many, many sixpences.

When the war ended, I turned my whole garden over to herbs. The scents in summer could make you drunken. They are sweet and wild and tangy. I branched into face creams, shampoos, eye gel, toner and body lotion. I still make them all myself, for employing others to do it would mean giving away my secret recipes. I did not advertise, but word spread, and now people from all over the world buy my products. The packaging has grown more sophisticated over the years. It was designed by Laura Dream Water who has a gift for art and colour. My Constant Water moisturiser costs over a hundred pounds a jar, but it works. I send it to a film star in Hollywood, famous for her flawless face. The tabloids say she has had thousands of dollars' worth of plastic surgery, but she hasn't. She uses my creams. My daughters use it. Their faces are young and supple, but not as smooth as mine. I use my cream myself, not that I need it – when you are One, age and wrinkles do not trouble you.

My products bring in an income. I'm not hugely wealthy, but money is not a worry. This is a relief to me, because earning a living when you are over one hundred and fourteen years old isn't easy. There is the pension. But when you have been claiming it for fifty-four years, government officials become suspicious. When you are one hundred and fourteen and look forty, they become even more suspicious. I stopped claiming it some years ago. Then, again, some firms have a policy of employing senior citizens. But when you write to Tesco or Sainsbury's telling them you are over a century old but of sound mind and able-bodied, they tend not to believe you. Their replies are somewhat negative.

My products took off in the sixties, when people were into natural things. It was a good decade for me. I let my hair fall round my shoulders and threw away my roll-on girdle. I loved the music. I loved everything that was going on. I took up with a folk musician who lived with me in an easy on-and-off way. I had four more daughters who were the first to be known publicly by their native names. They were my unbracketed ones. All my daughters before that time had their Indian names in brackets between their Christian and surnames.

How odd it is that after a child is born I soon forget the pain and sweat and cursing, and remember only the joy of feeling someone new slip into the world. And the exquisiteness of feeling that newborn skin on mine when my infant is laid by my breast. I also forget the guilt.

This is a torment. It sweeps through me every time I hold a new child in my arms. I am compelled to keep her warm, dry, happy, fed, amused and safe. I am driven. I weep. There is nothing I can do about it.

I had decided that Justine would be my last. Twenty daughters are surely enough. But the broodiness struck. I found myself longing to hold a baby in my arms, to kiss a damp and perfect forehead, to feel a tiny body next to mine and to smell that sweet, slightly vanilla, infant smell. I smiled to babies in the street, loomed over prams, swooned at infants' clothes in the shops. It is a longing I'm very familiar with. But I decided I would not give in to it.

Then, nine months ago, my gorgeous, wayward, youngest daughter told me she was going to a rock festival.

'You're too young,' I told her.

'But you went to festivals,' she said.

Indeed I did. Probably that's why I didn't want her to go to one.

She went on and on, every day pleading. And I always said, 'No.'

In a final ploy to get her way she asked if I would come with her.

'I'm too old for such things,' I said. 'Besides nobody wants to go to a rock festival with their mother.'

'I do,' she said. 'You're not like other mothers. Everyone says so.'

Ah, flattery. It'll get you everywhere – rock festivals included. I agreed. I went.

I refused to camp at the site and booked us both into a local B&B. But we went along every day and stayed till well into the next day. I didn't sleep much. The atmosphere was exhilarating, the noise deafening. Justine was ecstatic. And so was I. The whole experience was noisier and wilder than the festivals I remembered. People jumped and danced. The light shows were extravagant. I had a little twinge of nostalgia, wishing I was at the Isle of Wight listening to Jimi Hendrix. But that was many miles and forty years ago.

I met a man. Don't I always? He was younger than me, bright-eyed, quick-witted and handsome. His hair was black. I fell. Don't I always? I didn't sleep with him when we were at the festival. I was sharing a room with Justine. But two days after we got home, he turned up at my door.

We sat up late, talking. Talking and talking and talking in the candlelight, but I forgot to ask my important question. Did he have any brothers? And if he did, he wasn't the seventh born, was he?

He brought me a glass of Coke, which I refused as I only drink water.

'Go on,' he said. 'Drink something young. Get in touch with a different generation.'

So I drank. It fizzed through me, bubbles in my

throat. But I felt giddy and laughed. So he brought me another. And I drank. He kissed me. I took him to my bed. I was thinking of my longing, I was dreaming of a new child. Someone to hold to me when Justine went off into the world. I didn't want to be alone.

In the morning, when that bright summer light streamed into my window, I saw him properly for the first time. 'Your hair is dyed,' I said. It was a surprise to me.

'Yeah, I'm a natural blond. I went black a while back.'

'You are golden,' I said.

He winked and said, 'If you like.'

'What was in that drink you gave me?'

'I slipped a little something into it to make you happy. Whisky.'

Golden.

My voice cracked as I asked if he had any brothers.

'Six,' he told me. 'I am the seventh. I am a seventh son of a seventh son. Cool or what?'

I knew I was done for. My time was up.

He left soon after. He kissed me on the lips, winked and said goodbye. I do believe that as he walked up the garden path, he leapt in the air and clicked his heels. I realised as I watched him go that I did not even know his name.

My new ones will be born soon. I will have twins. A boy and a girl.

He will be the second born of the two. He will be golden. He will be an imp. He will win hearts, break hearts and cause mischief. He will have seven children but will not know any of them, and he will love none of them. I will have brought trouble into the world.

I am already getting old. My hands are gnarled, covered in brown spots. My hair is turning white; a huge clump fell out yesterday. My joints ache. I have lines round my eyes and mouth. My voice is cracked. It is going to be an agonising birth. I am not up to it. Soon I will be ancient. I will crumble away. I will look like the mother of mothers. A woman who has given birth to twenty-one daughters, and one son.

My girl, Mercy Breathing Water, will come into the world first, my twenty-first child. I look at it like this – she will be my third seventh child. She will be One. She will know the joy. And she will feel the guilt. I shall leave her a letter to be opened on her sixteenth birthday, warning her about the golden.

'Motherhood is a huge businesss. A man – or, indeed, another woman – may fulfil a whole range of needs and wants in a woman, but motherhood, whilst unquestionably fulfilling, is a whole new dimension in one's life, a whole new career, a whole new – and eternal – preoccupation.

There are, I often feel, only two relationships in life that you are completely stuck with: one with yourself and another with your children. And while I would champion to the death a woman's right NOT to have children (and, almost more, the right not to be pilloried for making that choice), those who do opt for motherhood, do go through the looking glass to a place from which no one ever completely returns.

You don't return because a) you can't and b) you don't want to. You can no longer contemplate life without that dimension.

It is visceral, it is absorbing and it is not – for once in this demanding multiple-choice life – a matter of choosing. It is also, and this is something you obviously can't see when you hold your first spit-new baby, endlessly evolving.

You are the baby, and then the child, then the adolescent, then the young woman and then the mother. At the same time, you are the daughter and the granddaughter. In time, you add being the grandmother to being the mother. At the moment I write this, I am a daughter, a mother, a grandmother, a stepmother and a step-grandmother. I belong, in the beat-in-the-blood sense, to four other females, who range in age from eight to eighty-seven. It is a far cry, in motherhood terms, from a blue-robed Madonna focusing with exquisite single-mindedness on her one swaddled baby.

But it is this diversity and evolution that makes motherhood, for me, so central, so enormous. I'm not the daughter I was at twelve; I'm not the mother I was at thirty; my children are not the children they were twenty years ago. But we are all, with equal or even greater validity, something else; we have moved round in the dance, and we can only be what we are now because of what we have been before.

And none of us, I think, can imagine a life without an opportunity – even if it's only in fantasy – for this crucial relationship in one of its many manifestations. It isn't just that, taking all forms and varieties, motherhood works, for society, for the human condition. It's also that it's so interesting, fascinating even. And, with a bit of luck, it lasts a lifetime …'

Joanna Trollope

Spinning Webs

Shyama Perera

My mum is pathologically scared of spiders. Inevitably, that fear transmitted itself to me.

One morning when I was fourteen we had a crippling domestic emergency. A common house arachnid was spotted lolloping purposefully towards the fridge. Petrified, I started screaming. My mother turned pale. Shoving me out of the kitchen, she slammed the door on the beast, sealing the edges with masking tape.

'Left without food, it will die.'

'But the kitchen's *full* of food, Ma!'

'It can't open cupboards.'

'But what about my breakfast?'

For three glorious days and nights we lived on croissants and Chinese take-aways, waiting for our many-legged friend to meet his Armageddon.

We were replete with fear.

As a Buddhist, my mother will not kill a living creature. Letting it die of natural causes, however, is fine. If anything, she was offering the chap a premature legs-up to reincarnation as a higher being.

The fourth morning, a glorious summer Saturday, Mum tentatively entered the kitchen.

Nothing.

I cheered as she stood bravely at the fridge. For a single second there was triumph. But then: out it charged! The Zola Budd of the insect world!

Within seconds I was barricaded on the balcony of our fourth-floor flat. Mum ran onto the communal walkway, calling for help. A bemused neighbour arrived. 'No killing!' my mother cried, giving him a paper bag in which to trap the beast.

I emerged as he left, laughing, with the spider in a bag. And I watched from the kitchen window as he went down the stairs and threw the bag into the communal incinerator where they burned the rubbish from our block.

A year later my hamster, Sexpot, met the same fate, though, thankfully, he was dead at the time.

Bored with a diet of seeds and evenings spent sleeping in the pocket of my mother's brown cardigan, he had a last run on the exercise wheel and expired in a small pool of blood.

Ma was inconsolable. 'He was like a son to me,' she wept.

I'd purloined Sexpot from the school animal house, after bringing him home for the holidays. He was family.

Once my mum was home from work, the two were inseparable. Now he'd popped his clogs; kicked the hamster bucket; begun his voyage across the Styx. Aiee!

Weeping as if the world had come to an end, she made him a burial casket – a scented silk-lined tissue box in which his gently wrapped body was placed.

On the green behind our council block, with the tomb of Sarah Siddons standing sentinel in the dark, my mother started digging with the fork and scoop that she used to plant tomatoes on our balcony. She dug. And dug. And dug. It was March. We'd had frosts for weeks. The earth had coalesced into an immovable mass.

The mission aborted, she and I processed sombrely back up the stairs to the same incinerator that had once consumed our spider. There, incanting Buddhist chants, she dispatched Sexpot into the iron darkness.

We were vegetarian for a week, as a mark of respect.

My mother, Mallika, grew up in rural Sri Lanka surrounded by abundance – coconuts, rice paddy, pineapples, jackfruit, mangoes, sugar cane ...

She charmed me, as she now charms my daughters, with stories of the squirrels and birds she tamed and trained when home from boarding school. But here, in the cold of England, there would be only one pet apart from Sexpot: her cat, Kurundas, Kuru for short.

Despite Mum's best endeavours, Kuru was beyond taming.

He was dysfunctional by day; a psychopath at night. When she made nocturnal visits to the loo, he'd claw her legs. She took to carrying a water spray to scare him off. But the scars remain.

Again I was part of the supply chain. I'd left home and acquired Kuru as a bedsit companion. Alas, within hours of his arrival, I was a sneezing, wheezy, rheumy-eyed wreck. I lodged him with my mother.

He lived at her side for nineteen years, terrorising visitors with his hissing and spitting. For the last year of his life, I lived with him too, as my mother and my family were then sharing a home.

For the first time, Kuru had a garden instead of a balcony, but he was scared of the feline oppos who stalked him with Single White Female tenacity. He was too old for change. He lost a tooth and couldn't eat.

That summer, he died in a basket by the Aga. For hour after hour my mother, small, stoic and solitary, sat at his side. Again, there was chanting. Six hours of it on tape. 'Let him go peacefully to his next life.'

After he'd died, she went outside. Aged sixty-eight and as slight as Kylie, this time her spade hit no resistance. She dug his grave, buried him, and planted flowers, which, I hope, still bloom each summer.

*

This makes it sound as if my mum's entire life has been devoted to creature avoidance or creature care, and in a way this is true, though the creature who remains at the centre of her world has proved more wild, scary and problematic than any others that have crossed her path.

I arrived when she was twenty-six and in Moscow, the wife of a young Sri Lankan diplomat – a woman in the invidious position of being a pregnant vegan in a country where potatoes were the only available vegetable.

'Change your diet or risk the baby's health,' she was told.

At the doctor's behest, my father pinched her nose shut and poured two pints of milk down her throat each morning. Even now the smell of it makes her retch.

It was minus twenty outside. The slight young woman from the tropics was ordered to stay fit for the birth. Weighted down by multiple layers of clothing, she'd attempt to go for walks and would faint in the street. Passing women lifted her sari to see if she had legs. Time and again, strangers carried her home.

Finally I arrived, the first Ceylonese to be born behind the Iron Curtain. My birth was reported in the Russian and Sinhalese newspapers, but that was no comfort to her as she lay in the labour room with no idea what was going on. Her Russian, while competent, didn't stretch to the finer points of obstetrics.

The babies were delivered in the order that the mothers had arrived at the hospital, irrespective of what stage each woman had reached. 'They were all screaming.'

My arrival, 8lbs 2oz and in a hurry, was terrifying for someone so innocent she didn't know the facts of life on her wedding night. Perhaps then, it's not surprising that the detail is erased from her memory. Suffice to say, the horrors of that day – 4th March 1958 – were nothing compared to what she's put up with since.

We pitched up in Paddington four years later. My father had resigned his job in the middle of a posting to Bonn and taken us back to Sri Lanka. Then he announced he was leaving for Germany to set up an accountancy business. 'I'll send for you once I've settled.'

Sensing something was wrong, my mum and I got on the next boat and followed him to London, where he'd disembarked en route to West Germany. 'Why did you come?' he asked crossly, collecting us from Tilbury.

Two weeks later he was gone. He flew to Bonn, leaving us in a bedsit on Craven Hill Gardens. 'I'll send for you once I've settled,' he promised. Again. But he settled with his mistress, a woman with whom he had fallen in love during our brief sojourn there. We wouldn't see him again for fifteen years.

It was the winter of 1962: the one that's in the record books for smogs and cold. One day we came across a bus conductor guiding his driver through the dense filth by walking ahead with a lantern.

The pipes froze. In our tenement, there were two toilets and baths used by up to thirty people and none of them worked. My mother was robbed.

They were grim times. She was thirty-one and had never worked in her life. We had just £80. It was sink or swim. Putting aside her pain, her pride, her disappointments and expectations, she got any job she could – folding freshly ironed table linen in the bowels of the Grosvenor House Hotel.

Through the High Commission, she made a friend who'd care for me after school. My mother was skeletal, less than six stone, and barely earned enough to cover the rent. She was undaunted. 'At least they give me one meal a day, so what's left can feed you.'

Food, of course, is vital to the mother–child relationship. A newborn baby's first feed is an iconic bonding moment. That nurturing tie lasts all our lives, the daily meal an expression of love. Even now I'm a big, brown blob hitting fifty, my mother is driven by that compulsion, the absolute need to keep her child alive and whole through food.

These days, Sunday lunch at her house is a much-anticipated treat and she cooks enough for an army. But she has triumphed, it must be said, after a series of trial-and-error attempts at the dark culinary arts. I recall her boiled ox liver and scrambled brains – a once-only culinary low – with horror. Her curries and stews, on the other hand, were and are, faultless.

When I was thirteen we got our council flat, but up till then we always lived in single rooms. (This despite my mum taking the civil service exams and getting an accounting job with the General Post Office.) The best room was on the top floor at 13 Craven Terrace. It had a double bed, an armchair, a chest of drawers, a sink, a wardrobe in one alcove and a two-ring Belling cooker, with grill, in the other.

In this room, which measured twelve feet by eight at its widest point, my mum made feasts for up to ten people at a time. She bought melamine plates with roses. And tiny gold-rimmed glasses for peach wine. Our guests perched around the bed and against the walls. There was endless talk and laughter.

On New Year's Day she'd be up early cooking milk rice. Using a teacup we stacked the rice in circular moulds, pausing to chip intermittently at a big lump of jaggery – the unrefined molasses sugar that provided a sweet counterpoint to the fire of her onion curry.

As the trail of visitors started late morning, she'd be greeting each with a pocket diary. 'It's good to give. Start the year as you mean to go on. If you give, you receive.'

*

We certainly received a lot in terms of kindness and return invitations. Without my even realising it, she had created a whole community around us. This makes my mum sound like a larger-than-life character. She's anything but. Extremely gentle and reserved, what she does is create a sense of warmth and safety where others can relax and let their hair down.

She rarely lets her own down. Indeed, for years she wore it in the severest bun. This she fashioned on the back of her head with the help of a circular hairpiece, around which she pinned her tresses, securing it in a net. Photographs show a young, unsmiling woman with hardship etched across her fine features.

As a child, I was acutely embarrassed by her visible formality. I'd cringe at parents' evenings and school shows, wishing she would smile so my mates could get a glimpse of the mother she became at weekends: pony-tailed and youthful in stripey slacks and a blouse.

Then we'd go window-shopping along Oxford Street for hours. 'Let's get out of this place.' Or we'd walk to the library, popping in on friends along the way, stopping to get our spices at Patak's on Westbourne Grove.

Early evening, my mum would pull on an old sarong and we'd sit on the stairs outside our room sharing a bar of Cadbury's Dairy Milk – a weekly treat to indulge the genetic sweet tooth.

But on Monday, the hair was up again. Over the

years, that bun became to me a totem of repression and regulation. It prevented her from letting go, for fear of losing what little she had left.

As my childish adoration and appreciation turned into the half-truths and resentments of adolescence, I associated it with her past – an eastern-ness that had pushed her into subservient roles, first as a daughter and then as a wife. Now she wanted me that way too!

One day, I took direct action. When, as was usual, she asked me to trim the ends of her hair, I cheerfully took a large hank in my hand and cut it to shoulder length. She has had short hair ever since.

While this liberation has unquestionably improved her self-expression around the family, my mother continues to be a very private person. I'll swap life stories with strangers, but my mother will extract the stranger's life story while giving little of herself.

She gathers endlessly interesting and salacious information, but unlike me, she refuses to extrapolate meaning from it to the point where she will state black is white. Silence, to her, is a virtue, but I see it as a pig-headed unwillingness to get involved. She is the worst gossip I have ever had the misfortune to gossip with.

And yet, it's because of her love for detail that I became a journalist: because of her obsession with newspapers that continues to this day. As well as buying her own papers, Ma raids my recycling bin for back copies of mine. Piles of half-read broadsheets are jammed under her kitchen table – so high that sometimes there's no legroom.

Upstairs are endless envelopes full of cuttings going back forty years – anything from strange stories to anecdotes and comment.

When I was growing up, she read *The Times* and, later, the *Telegraph*, cover-to-cover every evening. Her grasp of international affairs is impressive. If she didn't finish, the paper was kept until she did. Even in our little room there was a pile.

In the same way that the Beaverbrooks grew up with newspaper stewardship in their blood, I grew up with a lust for news copy in mine. At fifteen, I was writing reviews for the *New Musical Express.* Mum smiled on this as a good grounding – a way of introducing me to the rewards of industry. She was less happy when, on leaving school at sixteen, I enrolled for A-levels in English and Politics to become a real journalist. 'Join BT,' she counselled. 'With your brains, you can come straight in as an executive officer and work your way up.' I refused, joining London Transport to learn how to touch-type. She was mortified.

When, at eighteen, I took a huge pay cut to start as a news trainee, she brought home-made food and chilli burgers to my bedsit. 'I wish you'd get a real job with prospects.'

It was only five years later, when I joined *The Guardian*, that she forgave me. And gave up the right-wing press for the left.

We've never agreed on politics, and that's how it should be. Who wants to have the same world vision as their parents? With the exception of Harold Wilson, whom she adored, my mother has always been a true blue.

The year Mrs Thatcher got in, she and an upstairs neighbour were the only ones cheering at my regular election-night party. As an industrious woman, and a Buddhist, she believes you create your own destiny. She purchased shares in every denationalised industry, bought her council flat, and celebrated a new dawn in her adopted homeland.

Her heart, however, is still in Sri Lanka. As the island has succumbed to the violence and misery of civil war, she has wept for her people. Once, she dreamed of retiring there, as many of her single friends, those who came here as teachers, have done. That was before grandchildren. 'My place is here with you and the girls.'

When pressed, it's actually to her childhood that my mother would have liked to return. To the land, to nature, to the secure imprint left by her parents. Her childhood is a golden time in her memory, punctuated by boarding-school life where proselytising Irish nuns made her life a misery. In the end she rebelled. She started challenging them. And got expelled. 'I couldn't stand those hypocrites.'

She went through the same process after arriving in England, a country that was alternately familiar, fair and welcoming, and cruelly hostile.

Mum was bullied horribly at work. She was quiet and meek and foreign: the perfect target. Outside, racism showed itself in different ways from the 'no blacks' signs on doorways to Teddy boys and, later, skinheads.

There were some deeply unpleasant incidents. Until one magic day in the mid-1970s (post-haircut?) when Ma was in Church Street market with her little basket on wheels. A white woman hissed and insulted her while she was shopping. Suddenly the worm turned.

'I followed her all around the stalls, loudly questioning why she had said such a thing,' my mother reported, proudly. 'She kept trying to get away from me, but I stayed at her side. She couldn't answer.'

Since then, she has been fearless in taking on anyone who dares cross her. Interestingly, few do. Recently, in a supermarket, an elderly man ticked her off for checking all the eggs in a box, and exchanging those that looked dodgy. 'I told him he was a silly old fool and should spend his time on more important things. He raised his voice to me, so I shouted at him. He soon went.'

*

Dogged: that's my mum. But then she's had to be. Her life has changed and developed in ways she could not even have imagined when she, Mallika Wijesinghe, arrived in this world, surrounded by abundance, on 1st October 1931. One of ten children, only five of whom survived, she grew up expecting to marry, have a large family and be near her parents for the rest of her life. Instead, she married, left the country, had just one child, lived alone and never returned except as a visitor.

Her four sisters and their families remain in Sri Lanka. When you see them together, they're remarkably alike. But inside, she's different. The rebel. She alone struck out and chose, through pride, to see things through unaided when life went pear-shaped in the most painful way.

As her child, I've inevitably classified her as conservative and staid in comparison to me.

We were at loggerheads throughout my teens because she disapproved of my western ways. 'What time do you call this? You are turning into a woman of the night!'

We were at loggerheads during my twenties because she disapproved of my single life. 'What man will want a woman with purple hair? Time is marching on, you know.'

We were at loggerheads during my thirties: 'What terrible things are you teaching your children? Why don't you get a job and let me care for them?'

Even now, she'll drive me mad with her warnings to

'cover your neck', 'make sure the door's locked', 'slow down', 'don't eat that rubbish' …

But what I've realised over time is that this is her outer shell – the one formed through anxiety because so much in her life has not gone to plan.

Hidden inside my mother is a true pioneer. She happily gave up a limiting rural life to spread her wings abroad. She took a chance on a mercurial man that her parents mistrusted. She learned foreign languages and embraced foreign ways. She struggled alone, raised a child and, starting with nothing in a strange land, earned respect and modest riches.

I present, as pioneering and outrageous, someone who challenges the world. But all I challenge is social mores. I don't challenge my surroundings or my lifestyle or myself. I am surrounded by what I know and like best. We are polar opposites. My mother is the pioneer; the one who breaches boundaries. She will not accept failure.

For example: driving.

She started lessons in her late forties. It took nine attempts for her to pass her test, by which time those of us who had dared act as supervisory drivers were gnawing off our legs from fear. If you told her to turn right, she turned left. If you said straight ahead, she reversed. I've lost count of the number of cars she wrote off in her attempts, but some of the losses were spectacular, as have been all subsequent losses.

My mother is so small she sits on cushions to see over the wheel. She has no sense of direction. At one point she would start every journey from Kilburn Station – two miles from home – because she could navigate from there.

In her early driving days, she was often in trouble. Once, she was stopped by police for reversing down the hard shoulder of the M4 after missing the Heathrow exit. They arrested her on the slip road. It was palpably an offence, but she put on such a convincing display of innocence and embarrassment that she got off.

She has escaped numerous parking charges by dramatically pleading ignorance – including the time she absent-mindedly parked her car on a zebra crossing in Soho and went shopping.

It is only in recent years that I've come to appreciate my mother's acting skills. As well as using them to wriggle out of difficult situations, she employs them to dispatch people she doesn't like.

Not long ago a hearing-aid specialist came round, at her request, to test her abilities. I went along too. From the moment he entered the house he patronised her. So, she argued, completely straight faced, that hearing aids made deafness worse.

'She's very illogical,' I said, at one point.

'No, she's very smart,' he replied grudgingly. After an hour, driven to defeat, he left.

She employs similar tactics when canvassers turn up at her door. Gesticulating wildly, she declares in pidgin English: 'So sorry, sah/mudem, me no understand. Only working. Lady of the house not here.'

The house, in the sleepy north-west London suburb of Colindale, continues to be a safe haven for all her friends and for visitors from home.

'I'm happy to sit in the kitchen all day, looking at the birds in the garden and reading my paper,' she says. But when I phone, she's often on shopping trips with my various 'aunties' or on her daily constitutional past the police college and down by the airstrip.

I gave her a pay-as-you-go mobile for emergencies, but she rarely remembers it. It took her two years to use up the £50 credit. One of the rare times I've called and found it on was during one of her regular outings with my girls. She answered in a whisper: 'I can't talk, I'm in the cinema with the children.'

'Then why didn't you keep the bloody thing turned off?' I said crossly.

Ma is not naturally a cinema fan. She fidgets and gets bored. But she's become one over the years to keep my girls happy.

My only memory of her taking me to the pictures is going to the Rialto, Westbourne Grove, to see Hayley Mills in *The Trouble with Angels.*

'That'll be six shillings and six pence for you and four shillings for the little girl,' the woman said.

'It's too much,' Mum replied. 'We don't have it.' End of outing.

Hang about! There was one other occasion ... When I was about ten, my mum and a group of friends were wandering down Oxford Street. There was an adult cinema on the corner opposite Selfridges and they decided to see the film there.

'Children not allowed,' the cashier said.

'She's not a child, she's just very short.'

And so I saw my first X film. It was some kind of torrid love affair – erotic but not explicit. The only nudity was a topless woman, but I hid my face anyway – it didn't feel right, sitting there with my mum.

Especially given what a prude *she* was.

My mother was so anti anything to do with bodily parts – particularly male bodily parts – that I once tentatively asked if she was a lesbian. She is imbued with values from a bygone age, though her own life bears witness to their degeneration.

For her, sex happens only within marriage, and marriage is for life. As a result she is trapped for ever by my father's philandering: loyal to a marriage and a man, now long dead.

Every 9th May, she reminds me that it's her wedding anniversary.

'But you're divorced,' I say.

When I was young she had many admirers, all of whom she spurned. They confirmed and compounded her loveliness and occasional lightness of heart. And also her aversion to the Male Gaze.

Paradoxically, particularly given her disapproval of carnal allusions, she owned a recording of *The Perfumed Garden* despite us not having a stereo. She went to see *Hair* and *Oh! Calcutta!*, and a strip show in Soho with a friend and her husband; and she is one of the few people in this country to have viewed *The Story of O* before it was banned.

There are hidden depths to my mother that I cannot access, so any account I give is very much a daughter's view, with all the information blackouts and complexity of emotion with which that relationship is imbued.

We are chalk and cheese, light and shade, cold and hot, yet each bears the other's imprint. I see her in my feet, my hands and my children; hear her in my home-spun philosophising and cautionary lectures; smell her influence in my cooking – both good and bad.

She provides the moral framework that I alternately resist and uphold. She is the rock from which I am hewn.

I have always said of my mother that she would not just give me the shirt off her back, but the flesh. She is everything a mother is supposed to be – helping me to define who I am *not,* as well as who I am.

That's why, when my fourteen-month-old daughter ran squealing at the sight of a spider, I made a decision. After a lifetime of calling in friends to deal with passing arachnids, I decided it was time to beat the fear. I didn't want her growing up to be as daft as her mother. So I froze. I took a deep breath, laughed, teased her for being silly and distracted her while dropping a book on the creature, leaving the mess for her father to clear later. I have never run from a spider since.

But … my mother's ethical viewpoint held fast. I couldn't reconcile my actions with her beliefs; *my* beliefs. It was wrong to kill a living thing, particularly one that had done me no harm.

So, over the years, I taught myself to catch spiders with a cup and a piece of card, and let them out of the window. Now, I don't bother with them at all. When my girls squealed that a spider was hovering by the coat rack, I refused to move him. He was there three days. They soon stopped worrying. My mother saw it there, too. And she still babysat. Maybe we've all conquered that one together?

*

I am writing this in the summer of Ma's seventy-fifth year.

A few weeks back we went to see a friend of mine in Suffolk. My mother gamely helped load up the punt with a picnic and then insisted on taking charge. Just four foot ten, she stood at the prow and rowed us – because the punt pole had broken – two miles up river.

It was a beautiful day, very hot and still, broken only by country sounds – birds, dogs, the invisible breaking of twigs. In the morning we'd been to an agricultural show that had worn us out, but Ma had a second wind. For an hour she rowed us into and out of bulrushes and river-banks. At one point she risked decapitation, ferrying us under a low bridge while shouting to some youths on top. 'I'm a learner driver with two instructors.'

I had to wrestle the oar off her for the return journey, worried that she was becoming tired, but she wasn't. She took on the role of back-seat driver, breaking open a beer and singing. Frank Sinatra. *I did it my way.*

And she has, of course. Done it her way. That's what makes her so extraordinary in my eyes, but also a totem of motherhood everywhere.

Her life has not gone to plan. How many do? But as a mother, there were few options open to her – she had to get on with it or I went down with her. So she did get on with it. And she overcame all the odds. She made a new life for the two of us, believing it was best for me. Her child.

Is she perfect? Of course not! There are times when each of us could happily walk away from the other without ever looking back. But they're short-lived.

Thank you, Mum, from the bottom of my heart.

And thank you, all mums, because sometimes it can be a thankless task, can't it?

Recently I was given a fridge magnet of a woman with a baby and a little girl. It says, 'The first forty years of motherhood are the hardest'.

In that case, my mum's now reached the easy bit. Or has she?

Waves

Justine Picardie

So, I'm sitting on a beach in Cornwall with some of my family, watching the children jump over the waves that are much too cold for me, and wondering how I ever managed to do what they are doing, but I did, I remember it, when I was a little girl. My youngest son, Tom, is in the water alongside his cousins Lola and Joe, who are just about to turn eleven. Tom is twelve, on the verge of becoming a teenager, intent on catching up with my older son, who is sixteen (where did all the time go? How did it disappear, before I could clutch hold of it, vanishing before I could keep it close against my heart?). I'm looking at Lola and Joe, who have both grown so tall this summer, just before they start at secondary school, and I can't help but think of their mother, my sister Ruth. What would she say if she was sitting here beside me now?

Ruth died of breast cancer in September 1997, agonised by many things, not least the savage fact that she couldn't live to see her two-year-old twins grow up. 'They won't remember me,' she said, as we sat watching our children play together on another beach, silently aware of the days slipping past us on another August holiday, six weeks before her death. 'You'll always be part of them,' I said, trying to reassure her, but she wasn't convinced, and she turned her face away from mine, tears running down her cheeks, not wanting my sympathy as the shadows lengthened at the end of a summer's day.

Nine years later – nine whole years, hundreds of days, thousands of them, yet today it seems like yesterday – I wish I could tell Ruth about her children, and sometimes I do talk to her about them, when I'm alone, whispering under my breath. Lola looks just like Ruth – the same cloud of curly dark hair, the same quizzical eyes, and lean long legs, strong enough to take her anywhere. Joe looks more like his father, Matt, but he's got his mother's way with words, and a similar streak of determination, taking him headlong into the waves, headlong into everything.

They don't remember Ruth, and they don't call her Mum – that title is reserved for their much-loved step-mother, and it has been for a very long time. But even so, I know now that I was right when I told my sister that she would always be part of her children's lives, even in death, for death does not part them, nor could it, not entirely, anyway. She's there in the curve of their faces, in the sparkle of their eyes as they face the waves, as they face the future; and in the future she will also be there when they look into their past. Nothing can take that away from them, or from her. That's what I find myself thinking, as I gaze out to sea today, watching over the children. That's what I tell my sister, silently, under my breath, my mouth shaping the words, softer than the sea breeze, but I will go on telling her, as her children grow older, as I do, year after year after year.

Jeep

Another Mother's Son

John O'Farrell

My husband has this joke he always does. He says he's the governor of the whole state except the one little bit where he lives. Oh sure, all the big decisions are left to me. 'I think we need some different flowers down the drive next year.'

'What sort of flowers?'

'Oh, I really don't mind, honey, you decide, you're so good at that stuff …'

Boy was I flattered! 'You're the governor of the governor's residence, Mary,' he joshed for the hundredth time. Well, I don't know about that, we never had any elections in our home; we never held primaries to see who the dog and cat wanted to run the household. 'Vote Mom for less federal interference and the right to drink from the toilet bowl.'

Actually the dog is a case in point. I wanted an Afghan hound but Bobby wouldn't hear of it. 'Afghan!

Are you crazy?' he said. 'A militant Islamic dog? What sort of message would that send out?' No, the type of dog was strictly limited to breeds named after parts of the United States. I suggested a Boston terrier but Bobby was nervous about the 'Boston' label – he thought it might make us seem a bit New England old money. So finally we got a Chesapeake Bay retriever which he called Liberty – how corny is that? And now I have to stand on the porch shouting 'Liberty! Liberty!' like I'm one of those women in paintings of the French Revolution who fought for equality with their breasts hanging out. He was deadly serious about the whole dog package. You can't be too careful, he said – look at that senator whose teenage son named their cat Castro as a joke. When the press got hold of it he ended up losing his seat. So that's why we have an American breed of dog called Liberty – the only dog in town named after a feminine hygiene product.

Bobby got me the dog when the boys left home. For twenty years I was 'Ted and Scott's mom', and now Ted and Scott are both away at college and it's just me and a big empty hole inside me, that's supposed to be filled with a Chesapeake Bay retriever. He's a fine dog, though. I think he must be the one creature in the state who doesn't wag his tail at me just because of who I'm married to. Everyone else points me out and says, 'Let this lady to the front of the line, this is Bobby's wife, Mary.' So that's me; that's who I am; I'm not Ted and Scott's mom any more, I'm the governor's wife, I'm 'Bobby's-Wife-Mary'.

'What do you do?'

'My husband's the state governor.'

It answers the question without answering the question, which goes to show I could have been a politician too. But instead I am one of America's fifty-first ladies. No, correction, there are a handful of female state governors. I don't know what their partners are called. 'First gentlemen', I guess. When the National Governors' Association had its anniversary, we all got together for a big party at the White House and had our pictures taken with the President. It was like a political version of Miss America. I thought for a minute he might want to see us all again in our bathing suits.

I got chatting to Miss New York afterward – what a cow she was. She comes on all superior to me just because her husband is governor of a big famous state and my husband is only governor of a couple of million people. She was looking down her plastic nose at me and saying, 'Now where is it your husband is governor again – it's one of those square states in the middle, isn't it?' And her little neighbour, Miss Vermont, is standing next to her gazing up in admiration. 'So tell me, I'm fascinated …' she goes on. 'When your state was admitted to the Union, how did they decide where to put the borders? Did they just get a ruler out and draw a square on the map or what?'

'No …' I said, 'we just have very straight rivers …' and she took a second to realise I was joking.

The President was charming and asked me about my immunisation campaign. I told him all about how the mother of every child born in the state gets a congratulations card from me with details of why they should get their child immunised, and I told him how I had gotten Hallmark Cards to sponsor the whole campaign.

'Sounds like the perfect example of government working in partnership with private enterprise, Mary,' he said, and he shook my hand and I knew my forty-five seconds were up. I was really impressed he knew my name and what I'd been doing; it made me feel kind of special. Then, as I moved on, he was approached by the next governor's wife and I heard his aide whisper, 'Jessica Francis, West Virginia, homeless project.' I can't believe I was so flattered and taken in; why – I've whispered names in Bobby's ear a million times. But like Bobby always says, nothing is what it seems in politics.

Of course the immunisation thing wasn't my idea, it's just the sort of thing that first ladies do. I hope it saves some lives, but somehow I can't feel proud, it's not something I would have done if Bobby hadn't gotten himself elected. I'm kinda playing out a role that someone else has written: I'm doing what's expected. So I stand there with my husband, the two of us posing for the cameras either side of a giant model syringe. It's ironic, really, because injection is the method of execution that we have in this state. The governor's wife is trying to get all the poor kids injected to save their lives, while the governor's job is to give the final authority for lethal injections to end them. Soon after Bobby was elected he had to give the go-ahead for a guy on death row to be executed, and some student magazine cut me out of the photo and just had Bobby smiling and doing a big thumbs-up, with his other arm around the giant syringe. He was mad about that. He hates it when prisoners on death row lose their appeals. The whole state saying, 'What's the governor going to do; is he going to grant clemency or is he going to send a man to his death,' and it's all down to him, everyone's waiting on his answer and suddenly this is it; it's not choosing the flowers in the drive; he can't leave this one to me.

I don't know why Bobby went into politics, he's always hated making decisions. He breaks out in a sweat when I say, 'Honey or maple syrup on your waffles?' He has to make up his mind on a case this week. A seventeen-year-old drug addict, an Hispanic called Jose Alvaraz, held up a gas station, and a trucker came in, saw what was going on and tried to disarm him. Next thing, the trucker's lying dead on the floor. That all happened ten years ago but now the boy's an adult and he's lost his final appeal and Bobby has to decide if he should get the death penalty.

The case has been brewing on the news for a few weeks. I saw the boy's mother on TV again last night, crying and begging outside the prison, saying it was all her fault because her ex-boyfriend had kept beating Jose up, and I thought of my two fine sons off at college and there was her boy waiting on death row, and for a moment I wanted to go and stand outside that jail beside her, though I knew that probably wouldn't have been very appropriate. But she's just another mother like me. When my Scott was fifteen and robbed those beers and took that car, he could have killed someone, he could have ruined his own life that night. But I made sure my boy had an alibi, the insurance paid the damages to the shop, no one was hurt and now Scott is the golden boy about to collect his degree. If Jose's mom had concocted some story, would they have believed her?

Bobby knows I don't believe in capital punishment. 'It's always the poor people who get rubbed out,' I said to him. 'The US government never executed a rich white man.'

'I've got a crazy John Lennon fan keeps writing to me who'd disagree with you there, honey,' and we laughed about the green ink letters he brings home sometimes.

I went with Bobby last year when he was shown round the prison for the criminally insane. They had a sign on the wall in the prison workshop: *You don't have to be mad to work here, but it helps.* So at least someone kept their sense of humour. There was this huge dining room full of deranged people, all whooping at him and leering at me. It was a bit like the party convention, only no balloons. They were mainly murderers and rapists, though obviously you don't ask. I didn't actually talk to any of the inmates; it would be kind of hard to get the small talk going. Anyway these particular guys were certified lunatics, so whatever it was they'd done they couldn't be executed for it. In fact sometimes they try to kill themselves and the warders have to stop them. See, you're not allowed to execute a prisoner if he is clinically insane; you have to try and cure him; give him care and treatment, over years and years, with counselling and medication and all that stuff, and if the shrink does his job well and stops the guy wanting to commit suicide and he gets completely better, well, then you're allowed to execute him. Must be kind of hard for the prison psychiatrist to motivate himself sometimes.

We saw the other wing of the prison as well. The main part where they're not crazy, they're just getting that way waiting for their executions. Some of them spend fifteen years having petitions rejected and appeals turned down; half their lifetime wondering when they're going to be put to death, and that's not guaranteed to improve anyone's sanity. I'd say weaving baskets would only take your mind off it for a short while. They hated us in there because one of Bobby's election promises had been to ban smoking in all public buildings in the state, so now the guys on death row aren't allowed to smoke. We can't have them getting lung cancer. But all the officers made a fuss of me and treated me like I was real important because I'm Bobby's-Wife-Mary, but I think it was that visit that really started all my problems.

There was a guy in there who had murdered his wife, and his mistress as well just to keep things fair, and he looked at me and said, 'Ooh, look at the grand lady with all her gold rings.' I tried to cover up my fingers but I couldn't and Bobby put his arm around me, protective like. The prison welfare officer said, 'Don't go getting yourself in trouble, Casey,' which I thought was a strange thing to say to a prisoner on death row; I'd say he was in quite a lot of trouble already. 'How did you get to be such a grand lady …' Casey went on '… by screwing the state governor, that's how.' And then two prison officers jumped on him and wrestled him to the floor but he didn't stop. 'Salute the lady, she's important, she screws the state governor!'

Bobby said he should never have let me go round the jail, that he'd only gone himself because the civil liberties lobby kept saying he had no idea what it was like in there. But it was important I saw it, that I saw those prison officers knock that Casey's teeth out with their batons. It kind of makes you take notice of what someone is saying to you, when there is blood coming out of their mouth at the same time. Maybe that's why it stayed with me. Next time we went to an NGA function, I was looking at all the other governors' wives and I was thinking, 'They think they're all so special, but what have they ever done? They're important 'cos they sleep with the governor!' I couldn't help giggling to myself, looking at them all mooching around, thinking they're all so wonderful. Like Marie Osmond, only less self-aware. 'I'm chair of this charity, and I launched this literacy programme and I'm patron of this society …' God, it made me want to stand on the buffet table and shout out loud, 'It's because of who we married, you schmucks! Hello!? We're not asked to do all that stuff because of our special skills or some deep talent for fundraising that the charities have spotted in us. The only thing we achieved is to be married to the governor. What's so damn clever about that?' Except I wouldn't have said 'damn' 'cos Miss Utah was there, and she probably never heard that word before.

*

That prisoner on death row put into words what I'd been feeling ever since Bobby was first voted in as governor. He'd spent a year running for high office, so I had to spend a year running on the machine at the gym. Running with all my strength and not going anywhere; that just about sums it up. On election night I cheered and clapped and waved my little plastic Stars and Stripes, but inside I felt that though he'd won, somehow I'd lost. Like he was now so important we could never have a normal relationship again. Maybe it's like that for all politicians' wives. In the middle of the Cuban Missile Crisis, when John Kennedy was working day and night to avert all-out nuclear war with Russia, I wonder if Jackie got mad with him and said, 'Well, aren't you going to ask me what *I've* been doing?'

Bobby and I always end up fighting if I try to talk to him about this. He can't bear me to suggest that perhaps I am not the luckiest woman since Pocahontas. This morning I was very quiet and probably a little brusque, and Bobby smiled at me and I looked away and didn't smile back, and eventually he threw down his toast and said, 'So what are you in such a mood about?' I said that I wasn't in a mood, and then I put down my orange juice and nearly broke the glass.

'Come on, what is it?' he said, because I obviously hadn't sounded very convincing. I busied myself clearing up the breakfast things. I must have wiped the draining board five times.

The fight this morning followed our usual pattern. To begin with, we don't communicate one to one; somehow we've gotten into the habit of using the dog as a go-between. When Bobby can't get any response from me, when he's given up trying to address me directly, he'll wait until we're all in the same room and then he will tell the dog how unreasonable I am being.

'Well, Liberty, it seems Mommy is in one of her moods again!' he'll say, and the dog will cock his head on one side and listen sympathetically.

'Well, Liberty, if Daddy ever listened to anything Mom had to say to him perhaps she wouldn't get so mad.' And then the dog looks across at me and maybe wags his tail slightly.

'You know, Liberty, I reckon your mommy ought to try thinking about the sort of pressure I am under in my job and that maybe I don't need more problems piled up in front of me before I've even left for work in the morning.'

Liberty carries on panting and thinks about that.

'Ha! Do you know what, Liberty? I don't think your daddy has the slightest idea how many sacrifices *I* made when he went into politics. I don't think he's even thought about what it's been like for me since the boys left home and I'm here on my own.'

Poor Liberty is getting pretty anxious by this time. He's been glancing back and forth between the two of us, hanging on every syllable, but not one word we have said to him has sounded even remotely like 'din-dins' or 'fetch'.

'Well, Liberty, I think Mom ought to realise how lucky she is. If I hadn't worked so hard and put in all those hours, she wouldn't be living in this beautiful governor's residence; she'd still be typing out insurance claims back home in god-damn Milwaukee!' Bobby shouts the name of my home town with his usual contempt and the dog thinks, 'YES!! He said, *Walkies*! Now I understand what they've been trying to tell me,' and he barks and runs around in excited circles and Bobby shouts, 'No, Liberty! No, Liberty!' which is not the sort of thing you normally expect to hear from an American politician.

Now I'm angry enough to start talking to Bobby directly. 'Being married to you has held me back,' I snap at him. 'It's stopped me doing anything for myself, anything that *I* might have wanted to do.'

'Don't shout at me, Mary!' Whenever Bobby doesn't have an answer for something I say, then he just gets mad about the way I'm saying it. Like even if one day he went berserk with his hunting rifle and murdered all my brothers and sisters; if I dared criticise him for it he'd probably say, 'Don't call me a murderer *in that tone of voice.*' Sooner or later every fight shortcuts to the fact that I am raising my voice, so somehow we never have the fight that I want to have, like I came out dressed for ice hockey and suddenly we're on a baseball pitch.

Eventually Bobby responded to what I was trying to say. 'For God's sake, Mary, we've been over this. You are the governor's wife for crying out loud – the first lady of the state – how much more important could you be?' and then he segued effortlessly into playing the martyred victim of the piece, so a discussion about the fact that I felt unhappy turned into a reflection upon him being unhappy. 'Do you have any idea how much it hurts me to hear you say these things? I have worked every hour the good Lord sends to get us where we are today; but it isn't enough for you. Have you thought about how selfish that is, how worthless you make me feel?'

It was time to detonate my killer line, the one I'd prepared earlier. The sentence was: 'Why does everything come back to *you*. Can't you see, that just for once this isn't about *you*; it's about *me*.' Except I was so wound up by this time that I got my words mixed up; it came out all wrong. 'This isn't about *you* ...' I blurted out. 'It's about *you*.'

He paused. 'You said *you* twice,' he sighed, in his special patronising tone that he keeps in the glove box for when I'm map-reading. Even if he was right, by now I was so mad with him I wasn't prepared to concede a thing.

'No, I said it's about *me*.'

'No, you said the word *you.*'

'I said *me.*'

'No, Mary, you said "It isn't about you; it's about you." It doesn't make any sense.'

I knew he was right, but I had to front it out. 'I said *you* first of all ...' I explained. "This isn't about *you*," but then I said, "it's about *me.*"'

'No, you said *you* both times.'

'I said *me* second time.'

'You said *you.*'

'Me.'

'You.'

'Me.'

'You.'

I don't know if this is how Bobby wins arguments in the state legislature; it might explain why the debates always go on for so long.

'Oh this is ridiculous,' he finally declared. 'We talked about this before and it's always the same thing. You want all the benefits of me being governor, but you'd rather I wasn't out there doing all the work all the time.'

'At least when I was typing out insurance claims it was *me* doing it ...' I say. 'I got the job in my own right, because I passed the typing test, not because I was married to someone important.'

'Aren't you proud to be who you are?' he carried on, his indignation growing. 'Aren't you proud that your husband has achieved high office?'

'THEY ARE NOT THE SAME THING. Who *I* am and what *you* have achieved are not the same thing; can't you see that?'

'Don't raise your voice,' he spat angrily. 'Don't raise your voice at me ...' And we're back on this again, even though I know he will shout ten times louder in a minute. He curses and yells and throws things around the room. Good job he never argued like that at the candidates' debate, else he'd have wound up throwing crockery at his opponent when they disagreed about welfare reform.

'God, you are impossible, Mary!' he finally exploded. His face went bright red and he shouted two inches from the end of my nose, and then he threw his breakfast cereal on the floor, though the bowl refused to smash, which I think may have annoyed him even more. I was sobbing by now, but he carried on yelling all the same, while Liberty was rushing round our legs, wagging his tail and gobbling up all the golden grahams that were scattered across the kitchen floor.

It was getting close to the point where Bobby would storm off in the car. He always does this, though last time we fought I hid his car keys. I couldn't resist it: his jacket was over the back of the kitchen chair and I took the keys out of the side pocket and slipped them behind that hideous state centenary cheese plate. Sure enough, a minute or so later when we were still shouting at each other, he grabbed his jacket and stormed off. He must have thought it was going to look pretty dramatic with the car speeding out of the gates, but the effect was spoiled by him sitting in the driving seat for ten full minutes, going through all his pockets over and over again, and then slipping back into the house and looking through all his coats and pants. He really wanted to ask me if I'd seen his car keys, but the whole point in storming off was that he wasn't talking to me any more.

But this morning was a weekday and his driver was waiting outside in the governor's official car. If Bobby wanted to show how mad he was, he'd have to ask the chauffeur to speed up the drive and knock over the plant pots on the way out. I heard him slam the front door of the governor's residence and then he was gone and it felt like he was never coming back. I picked up his cereal bowl and put it in the dishwasher and wiped down the breakfast bar. I needed to clear my head so I turned on the TV. What's the first thing I see? A big picture of Bobby smiling out at me. Like it's not bad enough having a photo of Bobby with the President grinning at me every time I go to the john; now Bobby's watching me from the television as well.

'Decision day for the governor,' says the anchor. 'Governor Jessop has until three pm today to grant clemency to Jose Alvaraz, or else the convicted killer will be executed by lethal injection,' and they cut to some footage of Jose's mother holding a tatty placard outside the jail. She looks right at me. 'Please …' she says, an imploring look from one mother to another, 'please don't let them kill my son.' And then they cut to an advert for dental floss.

When they come back to the newsroom, the experts debate what legal and political factors will determine the governor's decision; they talk about precedents and public opinion but not one of them makes the most important point: that mother is doomed to lose her son because the governor had a huge fight with his wife this morning. I want to be in that studio and tell all those experts that they don't know what the hell they're talking about. I want to push that pompous anchorman off his chair and say to the camera, 'Let's be clear about this. I know Governor Jessop better than anyone, and I can assure you that there is absolutely no way he is going to grant clemency two hours after his wife called him a selfish shithead, OK?'

Because it's true. Whatever happened in the courts and in the state attorney's office, any hope that mother had of saving her son was snuffed out over our breakfast table. Once Bobby had lost his temper and tried to smash his bowl of golden grahams on the floor, Jose's fate was already sealed. He would be dead by the time Bobby returned home for our silent, awkward evening meal.

I grab my coat and the keys for the station wagon, and now Liberty just can't believe it. We always have our walk after breakfast and here I am just going out of the door and leaving him alone in the house.

'I'm sorry, Liberty, but this important. I know, to you your walk is more important but you have to try and see the wider picture here.' I screech down the drive and I pull out slightly too quickly onto the main road, and a car honks and overtakes me and the driver shouts, 'Are you trying to kill someone?' I'm normally such a careful driver but I'm still wound up from our fight and seeing the TV footage of that young man looking so sad and defeated by the world as he was led away in handcuffs from his final appeal. I have to get to Bobby before his legal team.

I didn't realise that I was breaking the speed limit until I saw the flashing lights in my mirror. I pull over and two Highway Patrol cops take an eternity to get out of their car and stroll over. They're all ready to book me, when I take off my sunglasses in the hope that they recognise who I am.

'Shoot! If it isn't the first lady of the state herself! Sam, get over here! Look who it is …'

'Why it's Bobby Jessop's wife, Mary!'

I figured if I can turn on the charm they might not give me a ticket and I can be back on my way in a hundred and twenty seconds max.

'I do apologise, Officer. I realise I was breaking the speed limit, I was in such a hurry to get on with my charity work I just wasn't thinking.'

'That's all right, ma'am. My wife will be so impressed when I tell her I met you.'

'Of course, I don't expect you to treat me different to any other citizen ...'

'No, that's OK, ma'am. All that work you do for good causes an' all, you're entitled to be in a hurry sometimes.'

'Well, that's real understanding of you, Officer ... ?'

And I give him the chance to give me his name so he thinks I might assist his chances of promotion.

'Officer Januscharevenski, ma'am,' he says, or some name like it; it was so long and unpronounceable that he never stood a chance of being recommended for anything by anyone. But they've let me off a ticket, even if it is because I'm Bobby's-Wife-Mary, and I'm more than ready to get on my way again.

'I'd like to thank you for that card you sent my wife,' says the other cop.

'Excuse me?'

'Amy Smithson, remember? She had a little boy last summer and you sent her a congratulations card. Mighty kind of you.'

'Oh, that's right – and details of why you must get your child immunised ...'

'I don't remember anything about that, ma'am. Amy never said anything about that …'

'Oh, well, er – it wasn't important,' I heard myself say as I restarted the engine.

'You mean like immunisation against diseases and stuff?'

'Er, yeah, that kind of thing. Your wife probably has all that under control …' I was glancing round to see if it was clear to pull away.

'No, I ought to get this down because if you took the trouble to write and tell us about it, I'm gonna make sure Amy gets it done.'

Then the other patrolman chirps up again. 'And would it be all right if I asked for an autograph for *my* Amy. Oh, I ought to explain; you see both our wives are called Amy. Isn't that a weird coincidence?'

'My wife's called Amy. And his wife's called Amy. Makes you think, doesn't it?' said the other one, and they asked me what I think the chances of that are, and by now I've realised it would have been quicker if I'd kept on my sunglasses and let them just give me a ticket.

Twenty minutes later I'm rushing into the governor's office and up to his secretary, who's on the phone crying to her mother or someone.

'Bobby's still mad, then?' I say. She covers the receiver with her hand and tries to pull herself together.

'Mrs Jessop? The governor's in a meeting.'

'Is it the legal guys?'

'Yeah, they've only just gone in. But he said he wasn't to be disturbed …'

'That's OK – he won't mind me …' But as I headed for the door, she looked like she might start to cry some more and I made a mental note to buy her some flowers once I'd taken Liberty for an extra-long walk.

Bobby is sitting at his big oak desk with the flags behind it. Three guys are sitting in smaller chairs facing him. He looks up and he couldn't have been any more surprised if Elvis Presley had walked through the door.

'Mary!'

'Gentlemen, could you excuse us for a moment?' I say, coolly. 'My husband and I have something personal to discuss.'

They turn to Bobby and he hesitates. 'Can't this wait, Mary?' he says, still looking mad at me. The lawyers look at me like I'm in the witness box. They seem like they don't want to leave. So I pause and bite my lip and say, 'I'm sorry but I have something urgent to discuss with my husband. It won't take a minute.' And they take an age to shuffle out of the room, gathering papers and sighing that this woman's 'urgent personal' matter is taking precedence over the Alvaraz case.

'I'm so sorry, Bobby, I'm so sorry. I don't deserve you, I swear I don't.'

He softens slightly but I'm not forgiven yet.

'You said some pretty hurtful things this morning, Mary ...'

'I didn't mean them. I'm sorry. I'm just jealous that I have to share you with all the good people of the state. They're so lucky to have you as the governor and I'm so selfish to want you all to myself ...'

'Did you have to interrupt my meeting just to come and tell me that? Couldn't it have waited?'

'You're right, God, you're so right – see, you just always know the right thing to do – and I'm so stupid coming in here and disturbing you and everything.'

And before long we're friends again, and he thinks I'm emotional and ridiculous, but I've told him how much I love him and he looks a whole lot happier now. He senses he can't just shoo me out of the office after all we've been through that morning, so the legal team are kept waiting in the lobby and we talk a little while. I have some new photos of our Scott I got in the mail and I tell him he has been selected for the college soccer team.

'Soccer?' says his pa nervously, worried how that might play with the voters. 'Are you sure it wasn't football?'

We talk about how the boys are getting on, and I say I'm still learning to get by without them at home and for a moment he almost sees that their leaving must have been kind of hard for me. I remind him of how much we used to worry about Scott. About the time when he got drunk and stole and crashed that car. Bobby went deadly serious and whispered, 'No one must ever know about that, Mary.'

So I changed the subject completely.

'What are you doing this morning, honey?'

'Didn't you see it on the news? The Alvaraz case. He's due to be executed today.'

'God, it seems so unfair. He was only a kid when he killed that guy. Seems wrong that a man should die for something he did as a boy.'

'Well, the law is the law, honey.'

'I thought you had the final say.'

'Yeah, but I have to think about public opinion and rising crime an' all. Besides, he's nothing special; there's seventy, eighty child offenders on death row across the country.'

'Well, I just thank the Lord our Scott never ran anyone over in that car or else he'd probably be on death row as well.'

'That wouldn't be murder one, honey. Besides I don't want you ever talking about that again …'

'I'm sorry, honey, I promise. And I promise not to shout at you or complain about things when we're so lucky to have the life that you've worked so hard for … and of course I'll come with you to the NRA dinner-dance on Saturday week. It'll be fun!' And finally he hugs me and I kiss him and we hug some more.

'The people of this state don't know how lucky they are. To have a governor who chooses to do the right thing rather than whatever's popular ...'

'Well, sometimes they can be the same thing ...' he stammers anxiously.

'Why don't you come home from work early and we can have a big steak and a nice bottle of wine, eh? And strawberries and cream for dessert. And I won't even mind if you have a cigar as long as I can open a window.'

'That's OK, I don't mind smoking it out on the terrace ...'

'No, smoke it in the house ...'

'No, it's OK, I'll smoke it on the terrace ...'

'No, smoke it in the house ...'

'NO, I'LL SMOKE IT ON THE TERRACE ...' And we're that desperate to be nice to one another, we nearly end up fighting over this.

He says I'd better go and I leave one of the pictures of Scott on the desk and kiss him goodbye.

And then I return home and wait for the lunchtime news. Eventually they go live to the governor's press conference and there is Bobby walking out in front of all the reporters and photographers, and he looks nervous, but not as nervous as I feel because from looking at him I have no idea what he's decided to do. He pretends to contemplate for a second to demonstrate the gravity of the moment and then starts to speak.

'In September 1996 Jose Alvaraz did a terrible thing. He took the life of another man.'

My stomach feels heavy. This is not the speech of a forgiving politician.

'When Alvaraz did that, he knew that the penalty for murder in this state was death.'

He lowered his head, looking sombre and sorrowful, like the doctor who told me that Mother had died. 'When you elected me I promised I would be tough, and tough I will be.'

'Oh God, no,' I hear myself say out loud, but then his pause is too long.

'... Because going against public opinion on this case is one of the toughest things I ever had to do. There is no excuse for what that seventeen-year-old did on that terrible day in 1996. But no man should die for something he did as a boy. For this reason, I am granting clemency to Jose Alvaraz.'

I let out a huge cheer all alone in my kitchen. 'Way to go, Bobby!' I jump about punching the air, but Liberty is still so disgusted with me he doesn't even look up from the basket. Then the TV cuts to Jose's mother hearing the news and she screams and sobs and yells, 'Thank you, Jesus, thank you, Mary,' though I don't think she actually meant me. She has to be kept on her feet by her friends, and she holds up a tatty photo of her son to the TV camera and cries, 'Thank you, sir – thank you. My Jose was such a good boy when he was little, he was such a good boy, oh thank you, thank you, thank you …' And she is crying so much it's hard to hear what she is saying, but I feel the tears of relief burst forth from in me as well, and I think of my two sons that have been taken from me, my little boys suddenly grown up and gone to university, and I love them so much. Oh, Mrs Alvaraz! I think I can imagine how you must feel today, and then I sob for how happy I am that her son hasn't gone and how sad I feel that my two sons have.

The little boy in the photo is only ten or so and smiling, and doesn't know how wrong his life is going to go. But today he still has a life, it isn't going to end at 3 pm, it wasn't all heading towards a lethal injection on this sunny Tuesday in October. He will go to sleep tonight and wake up in the morning. He'll get a visit from his mother and they will touch their fingers against the glass and he will see the look of love in his mother's eyes; he will get letters and read books, and maybe one day he will be released; and if his mother's still alive, they can take a walk together in the park and sit on a bench and just talk a while.

And the only reason he is still on this earth is because of me, because of something I did. No one will ever know this; only I understand the forces that were at work during the most important few hours of his life, and it will always be my secret. But I know, I know I made a difference. And it makes me feel important and like I deserve that special seat in church, and the best table in the restaurant;, and I deserve that applause I get when I walk into the school room and the salute from all the soldiers in the army camp. Why – I'd say saving lives, anyone's life, is a special thing to do so it makes me feel like I have achieved something in my own right.

Because I knew Bobby had to make that decision today. But if we'd had a normal breakfast time and I had kissed him goodbye as he went off to work, then he never would have listened to me. We had to have a fight first. That was the only way to make Bobby want to give in to me; that was the only way to save that young man's life. I'm accompanying my husband to the Women in Business Charity Gala this evening and they've asked me to give a short speech. I'm going to tell them how proud I feel, how very proud. They'll smile and Bobby will smile, but I'd better not tell them my reasons why. Like Bobby says: 'Nothing is what it seems in politics.' There's another case coming up in the New Year. It has to be worth a try.

‘Being the mother of my daughter and son is both an eternal pleasure and an enormous privilege. No other achievement in my lifetime could top bringing them into the world and into my life, and I treasure the time I have with them – whether we’re belting out Broadway show tunes together or niggling over getting homework done!’

Dr Tanya Byron

My Mother

Stephanie Calman

As a child, I took the fruits of my mother's imagination for granted. Didn't everyone's mum tell them elaborate stories at bedtime, made up of a mixture of Greek myths, folk tales and the plots of operas? Didn't all children get home-made cards, painting sessions on the floor with giant bottles of paint and a choice of ten sizes of brush? Wasn't it entirely normal, at Hallowe'en, to invite all the neighbours' kids round and paint their faces green, or black out their teeth with mascara, then run round the neighbourhood 'scaring' passers-by? Not then, and not now. Trick or Treat is a soulless imitation of the saturnalia my mother brought with her from Scotland and inflicted on Bloomsbury's bemused residents. By the Christmas, when she put in our stockings tiny postboxes she'd made us out of spice pots, filled with handwritten, two-inch-long letters, we were beginning to realise she might just be a tiny bit unusual. '*Dear Lord Smythe*,' said one of them, headed St Narkover's School: '*We regret we must ask you to remove your son from the school and enclose the bill for costs incurred during the autumn term.'* Items included '*£3,428, gambling debts*', '*£2,000 to rebuild gym after fire*' and '*£150 for Matron's abortion*'. There was also a voucher in another envelope addressed to me, for '*£5 off your next diamond tiara*'.

This was not, as you may imagine, a woman who dwelt long on the challenges of ordinary domestic life. I can't remember ever seeing her do any housework. For some years we had a nanny who doubled as housekeeper, which was one reason. But in any case, cleaning was not something she felt was a good use of one's time. If you're dusting, I believe her reasoning goes, you're not having a conversation or reading a book. So, just as a small television for some people indicates they're intellectuals, for her it's mess. Clutter proves you have your mind on Higher Things. And she has. When we visit, I clean the kitchen while she flings theories and observations into the conversation which vary from scraps of Freud and Darwin to hilarious headlines from her local paper, and bits from books and poems she read sixty years ago. She then burrows amongst the crumpled brown paper bags and the overstuffed fridge and produces a meal. I harrumph at her for sometimes doing it in her overcoat or a weird multicoloured jumper, but generally while helping myself to seconds.

These days, to accommodate sons-in-law and grandchildren, she has made one concession to convention and accepted a sofa. But in the past she would never have one, nor an armchair. To watch TV we sat on her bed. When my sister and I outgrew our shared bedroom – each needing somewhere private to snog our boyfriends, she gave me the sitting-room.

'It'll be like three bedsits!' she said. And sure enough, our relationship took on a more flatmate-ish quality. Guests for dinner, whether ours or hers, were crammed round the table in the oddly shaped kitchen, the result of an imaginative conversion in which most of the middle had been scooped out to make the bathroom. We continued to watch TV on her bed. It was the closest I ever came to being a student.

In any case, despite her powerful intellect, she had no truck with parents whose love is conditional on A grades. It was she, not us, who complained about the amount of homework we got.

'I just think it's too much,' she'd say, shaking her head. Luckily, the school made up for it in ways of which she did approve: no uniform, no discernible rules and alongside the emphasis on Oxbridge, a leaning towards groovy self-expression. She thought it perfectly acceptable that grammar school girls should spend their lunchtimes dancing to Elvis records and organising beauty contests. When the big Biba store opened in Kensington, I wasted yet more of my youth trying on every tester at the lavish make-up counter and coming home liberally doused in an eye shadow called Midnight. This too was fine.

We weren't best friends during my adolescence – far from it. We had some pretty heated encounters over the inevitable effect of the school's liberal clothing policy, notably my attempt to copy the 'gipsy look' which briefly swept the nation in about 1976. My ensemble of off-the-shoulder blouse and white Victorian petticoat was pronounced evocative of the oldest profession, and I was pulled back from the doorstep and made to change. She got her own back by coming to collect me in gold sandals and a kaftan.

There was also a hideous row when, after a series of clashes with my French teacher, I announced I was giving the subject up. Having lived in Nantes after the war, where she designed window displays and adored everything French – including her boss, Mum was distraught. It was the one time she got my father to come over and tell me off.

But, as we headed towards the choppy waters of A-levels, she showed once again that an unusual mother was worth ten usual ones. In the holidays I had temped as a secretary. But instead of getting an early warning of how grim the world of work was for the average unqualified female, I let the wages – so much greater than pocket money – go to my head. School was just too *immature* for me, I decided. Anyway, I couldn't *stand* any more exams, so I wasn't going back for the sixth form. This would throw your normal middle-class parent into a seizure, but she didn't panic.

'Well,' she said. 'There are some really good books on the English list. Why don't you stay on and read them? You don't have to take the A-level if you don't want.' I did, *and* suffered French with Racine and his deadly, seventeenth-century rhyming couplets – though only because it was my other least-bad subject, not out of loyalty to her. But she didn't mind, didn't care about the grades, didn't pour all her hopes into my going to university and never used me to fulfil her ambitions. She had horrified her teachers by going to art school, had left the genteel bit of Glasgow for London, then run the fan club for a jazz band before getting a job on a magazine. She even lived with a man before marrying my father. She gave up full-time work to become a mother – a waste, I always felt, of her prodigious talents. But the lesson of her life, and her most precious gift to me, is that in order to be happy, you must live the life that's right for you. Everything else leads to misery.

She only tried to 'fit in' twice that I can remember. When I was fourteen she made a cake for my birthday. It didn't rise, and I had to reassure her that it didn't matter. Then, when I got married, she bought a traditional 'mother of the bride' outfit, a patterned two-piece that she nicknamed the Lady Mayoress kit. None of us liked it, and were relieved when she returned to normal. Her normal.

Harry Stone and the 24-Hour Church of Elvis

Joanne Harris

What would Elvis have done? That's a question that's often helped me through hard times; difficult choices; moral dilemmas. Sitting on a crowded train, people standing; woman gets on, might be pregnant, might not – hard to tell under the acres of pinafore – sandwiched between a kid in a Burberry baseball cap and an old lady with some Tesco's bags. Me, I've got my guitar case, I'm knackered from last night's show at the Lord Nelson and I ask myself: what would Elvis have done?

Well, apart from the fact that he wouldn't have been on the train to Huddersfield in the first place, it's pretty obvious. So I get up, don't I, with a smile and a suave gesture (only slightly marred by the guitar case bashing into the grab-rail). The kid behind me sniggers; the old lady with the shopping gives me a dirty look, like it should have been her; and the maybe-pregnant woman plops down without a word of thanks and opens a bag of smoky bacon crisps. Ignorant cow.

I was telling all this to Lil, half an hour later, in the Cape Cod chippy. Fishcake Lil, my number one biggest fan (and agent in the field); sees everything, knows everything that's going on from Malbry to the village, which is a serious bonus to someone in my line of work.

'What a shame, love. I'll put you some more scraps in, shall I?'

Elvis would – I decided against. 'Better not. Gotta be fit in this business, Lil.'

Lil nodded. She's a big girl, with a smooth, powdered face and long brown hair. Works at the chippy four days a week, and does tarot readings down the pub on Thursday nights under the name Lady Lilith. So she understands showbiz, which is a relief, because let's face it, most people have no idea of the strains and demands involved in being a top Elvis act.

'Good gig last night?'

'The best.' Actually it was a bit rough; there's a new crowd at the Lord Nelson, and you can see they're not used to class. One of them – a tall, skinny bloke in a torn-off T-shirt that made him look a bit like Bruce Springsteen – kept shouting 'Stand up!' and making comments like 'This un's only half! Does that mean we get half us money back?' I had a go at Bernie (he's the compère, goes under the stage name of Mike Stand), for not building me up enough during his intro. I know I'm on the short side, I told him, but the King himself wasn't that tall, it's the camerawork that does it, and besides, it's all a question of attitude. At which Mike said he was pretty bloody sure that Elvis had never got down off stage in the middle of a number and twatted a member of the audience just for saying 'I'll have half'.

Fair's fair. I over-reacted. Still, you'd think that six months of incident-free performances would have counted for something.

'To be honest, Lily,' I told her, splashing vinegar on my chips, 'I've been thinking of moving on. There's other places than the Lord Nelson, you know. The Rat, for instance.'

That was the Ratcliff Arms, the roughest pub in Malbry. I'd played there once, years ago, fifty quid a night and all of it danger money.

Lily's face fell. 'He's not sacked you?'

'Course not.' I gave her my 'Jailhouse Rock' look over my turned-up collar. 'I just wanted something a bit nearer home.' I lowered my voice. 'For professional purposes.'

Her eyes widened. 'You mean ... ?'

'Uh-huh.' Lily knows better than to mention it openly in the shop, with people coming in and out all the time, but she's the only person (apart from my clients, of course) who knows my secret. By day (and on Wednesday evenings) all Huddersfield knows me as Jim Santana, Top Elvis Act (pubs, weddings and private parties considered); but by night I walk the city streets as Harry Stone, lone gumshoe and private investigator, scourge of the criminal classes and one-man crusader against vice in all its forms. If you have a problem – and if you can find me (try the *Thomson* local or that little notice board in Malbry Post Office) – then I will solve it. Remember the Raj Fruit & Vegetable grocery job? That was one of mine. Mr Raj thought he could get away with buying raisins at the wholesaler's at fifty pence a pound, then soaking them, repackaging them and selling them at one-twenty for a small punnet under the label 'Jumbo Ready-To-Eat Raisins'.

But he hadn't counted on Harry Stone. I reported him to the Weights and Measures, who sent a strongly worded letter by return of post. Sorted. He won't be trying that scam again in a hurry, I can tell you.

Then there was Darren Bray, of Bray's lumber yard, with that van with the out-of-date tax disc parked on the road. And that John Whitehouse, claiming his dead dad's DSS benefits while his mum built that extension to their garage without informing the planning council. And Mrs Rawlinson in the snack bar down by the Methodist church, labelling her cheese and pickle sandwiches 'Suitable For Vegetarians' when she knows full well that neither the cheese nor the margarine have been approved by the proper authorities. That was an Advertising Standards job, and it took me a week of sitting there with my digital mini-camera, waiting for deliveries and drinking Mrs Rawlinson's milky tea. But I got there in the end. I always do. For the community. For myself. And for Elvis.

Having said that, the pay isn't always that good. Most of my income still comes from my act, but every good investigator needs a cover, and mine's as good as they come. In my line of work, I get around; I get to know people; and, of course, I have my informants.

Lily, for example. Fishcake Lil to most (Lady Lilith on Thursday nights, and by appointment). She glanced quickly over her shoulder to check that no one could overhear, then whispered: 'Who is it?'

'Brendan Mackie. Football coach for Malbry Miners.'

Lil had a think. 'Big bloke. Bit of a temper. Likes a drink. Always has haddock, chips, two scallops, battered sausage – always makes the same joke about the sausage ("not as big as some, love, but then it's got a lot to live up to"); wife sometimes comes in with him. Gail. Stripey blonde; perma-tan; bit tarty; gay brother works at B 'n Q; diet Coke; never wants batter on her fish.'

'Perfect.' I told you she was good. I looked around, but the shop was empty, and the only person I could see outside was Mr Menezies eating his chips by the bus stop, with his hearing aid turned off to save the battery. 'Between you and me, Lil, she's the target.'

'What, Gail?'

I nodded. 'Had a word with Brendan the other night. After-the-match gig at the Golden Cock. We got talking, as you do. He thinks she might be playing away.'

'He hired you?' said Lily.

'Uh-huh.' Well, nearly. What he'd actually said was: 'I'd give a lot to know what she gets up to when I'm at footie'. But an investigator has to read between the lines if he isn't to blow his cover. I reckoned I could charge him a tenner a day, plus expenses, if I got a result. It wasn't much, I know, and I was dying to get my teeth into a real crime and not just a marital, but I figured that if Brendan Mackie did find out that his wife was cheating on him, I'd be at the head of the queue to solve the murder.

Brendan Mackie. Lily was right. I can just about make it to five-five, if you count the quiff and the cowboy boots, and he towered over me even though he was sitting down and I wasn't. He was pleased with the act, though; told me he hadn't laughed so much since Granny got her tit caught in the mangle, and bought me a drink.

'So. D'you enjoy it then, this Elvis lark?'

'Uh-huh.'

'Z'it pay much?'

'It's all right.' I sensed from the start that he wouldn't understand the subtleties; the costumes; the lights; the exhilarating glamour and freedom and thrill of life on the road.

'Is Jim Santana your real name, or is it, like, a noom-de-ploom?'

'It's my real name,' I told him. 'I changed it by deed poll in 1977.'

'Crucial.' He swigged his lager for a moment, while I did the same to my rum and Coke. 'I suppose it's all got to be genuine, like, for your act. Like them trannies you get in Amsterdam. Twenty-four-seven, eh? I mean, there's no one going to take it seriously if you're a regular bloke all day and at night you're Elvis.'

'Uh-huh-huh.'

'That slays me, it really does.'

We talked awhile. I was halfway through the set, two costume changes in and two more to go. I do all the hits: 'Love Me Tender'; 'Jailhouse Rock'; 'King of the Road'. People love it, specially the older ones; it reminds them of the time when they were rebels. Nowadays it's hard to find anything worth rebelling against. It's all been done. Nothing's new; and however bright you burn – your Kurt Cobains and your Jim Morrisons – you're all going to end up in the same old hotel room at the last, doped and desperate. Except for Elvis.

I've got a shrine to him in my living room, you

know; with photographs and album covers and figurines. Lily calls it the '24-Hour Church of Elvis'. Not that I think he's God, or anything like that; but he's my inspiration. My idol. My muse.

I tried to say as much to Brendan Mackie, but I could tell it wasn't getting through. Waste of time, really. The more he drank, the more he wanted to talk about his wife. And so I let him; and I watched the case unfold.

Consider the suspect. Gail Mackie. Thirty-two. Married nine years, no kids, no job. Bored witless – I would be, if I was married to Brendan – nothing to do all day but take baths and have my nails done, and go to the Body In Question for Pilates and lunch. Was she cheating? It sounded likely. Everything fitted: the furtive manner, the unanswered mobile, the evenings out, the late-night showers as Brendan lay in bed. A doting husband, he'd never confronted her. Gail had a temper, so Lily said, and I guessed that Brendan would accept nothing less than photographic proof. Finally, I thought, a job worthy of Harry Stone.

'When do we start?' said Lily, her eyes brightening.

That *we*. Her and me. If only I could. But it's a proud and lonely thing to be a professional gumshoe and Elvis impersonator, and if my enemies ever found out about Lily and me …

'I can't afford a partner, Lil,' I said, not for the first time. 'Work in the shadows. In and out.' I demonstrated, using my chip-fork as a weapon. 'You'd only slow me down if it came to a fight, and if ever anything happened to you—'

'Oh, Jim,' said Lil softly. 'I wish you'd let me help.'

I gave her my 'Love Me Tender' look. 'Sweetheart,' I said. 'You've done enough.'

Well, that was the first stage done and dealt with. Now to confirm the client's suspicions, obtain photographic proof of his wife's infidelity and, finally, cash in on a job well done. I reckoned it might take me a week or so – say, ten days, plus expenses, we might be talking about a hundred and fifty quid or thereabouts, not bad at all, and a lot easier than the Lord Nelson on a Saturday night.

My first job was to locate the target. Easy enough, that, I thought. As it happened, there was a match that day, so I just turned up outside the house with my mini-camera and waited. It was cold for September; I wore my mac belted tightly with the collar turned up and walked around a bit to keep warm. Gail finally came out at three o' clock, ten minutes after Brendan left the house, carrying her gym bag and swinging her ponytail like a schoolgirl.

Bugger. She was taking the car. A little Fiesta. That stumped me a bit – I don't actually own a car at present (the last one got written off during problems associated with a previous case), and I had to do some quick thinking. Had to abandon the idea of leaping into a cab and driving after her – no cabs on Meadowbank Road – and although the number 10 bus was just coming round the bend at the time, I knew I couldn't count on the driver to accept my authority to commandeer his vehicle. In the end I had to sprint back down to the Cape Cod and borrow Lily's Micra, by which time Gail was long gone and the trail was growing cold.

I played a hunch, though, and followed her to the Body In Question, the local gym, where I managed to get in a couple of candid snaps just as Gail was coming out of the ladies' changing room. After that I went into the sports shop alongside, invested in a pair of swimming shorts (six quid, plus the swimming cap), and parked myself in the spa pool next to the glass-fronted Pilates studio, where I was able to watch the target's every move in comfort and security.

I'll give her this: she's an athletic girl. An hour's Pilates, followed by half an hour on the rowing machine, half an hour's swimming, half an hour's step class, a shower, and then – bingo! – a tall skinny de-caff latte in the gymnasium juice bar, in the company of a young man in a muscle shirt and a pair of Lycra running shorts.

I was out of the pool in a flash, showered and dressed before she could order a refill. It took a little longer than I'd first expected (in my haste I'd forgotten to buy a towel), but even so, I managed to find a seat not far from the couple, where I could snap a few more incriminating shots and, hopefully, tape their conversation using the mini-digital recorder in my pocket.

I ordered a Coke. The girl at the counter gave me a funny look – well, I don't go swimming very often, my quiff gets wet – and charged me two quid. Lucky for me, the case's open and closed. Two quid for a glass of Coke! Perhaps I ought to make that the subject of my next investigation – besides which, the Coke tasted distinctly watery. I made it last, though, all the time straining to listen to what Gail and Lycra Boy were whispering to each other, but I'd been in the pool for much too long; there was water in my ears, and I couldn't hear a bloody word.

Perhaps that was what caused me to drop my guard. That, or someone had been stalking me – causing the hunter to become the hunted in a bizarre quirk of fate. In any case, Gail was getting suspicious; I caught her watching me a couple of times with an odd look on her face, and once Lycra Boy turned round as well, and fixed me with a stare of such naked aggression that a lesser man might well have been intimidated.

Not me, though. Not Harry Stone. Instead I stared him out, lifted my glass and toasted him silently in watery Coke, so that Gail looked quite upset and got to her feet, and Lycra Boy took a step towards me, then saw my steely gaze and thought better of it, turning tail and legging it through the swing doors towards the car park and Gail's Fiesta, parked (illegally, I noticed, and with a wing-mirror misaligned) in an executive slot.

I tailed them back to the Mackie residence and parked the car at the bottom of the road, opposite the Cape Cod. Lily was just closing (she does bar work at the Rat on a Saturday night), and she smiled as she saw me coming. 'All right, Jim?'

Jesus, my cover. 'Harry,' I hissed, handing her the keys.

'Oh. Sorry, love. How d'it go?'

'Elvis himself couldn't have done a better job. Look at that now.' I glanced down the road at the Mackie house, all lit up now with the curtains drawn, and the target and the suspect alone in the sitting room, doing God knows what. 'Probable cause, they call it on TV. Means I can snoop around there as much as I like, though I do draw the line at breaking and entering.'

'Be careful, Jim.' Lily's eyes were wide. 'Don't want to get caught, do you?'

I grinned. 'You'd have to get up pretty early to catch Harry Stone with his pants down, Lil.'

For some reason, she blushed. 'I'll come with you. Keep watch, like.'

'Sorry, Lil. This is strictly a one-man job.'

Down by the Mackie place, I had another piece of luck. They'd left the curtains open a crack, and I could see straight into the living room. I reached for my camera. The room was deserted – I reckoned Gail and her fella had gone into the kitchen to make coffee – but there was a nice comfy sofa in front of the window, all lined up for a piece of illicit action, and my instincts told me that it would soon be occupied.

So I stood there for a while, watching and waiting. It was cold; it had started to rain and I could feel water trickling down the collar of my mac and into my boots. Still, it's a piss-poor P.I. who lets a bit of rain get him down, and besides, I was already wet from the spa pool. But I'd got a gig at eight that night – or rather, Jim Santana did – and by then I could tell my quiff would need some serious remedial work before I could call myself a top Elvis act again.

Still, in the line of duty, and all that. I must have been standing there for about fifteen minutes, getting colder and wetter. Then, bingo! The target and the suspect strolled into the living room, both carrying coffee cups, and sat down together. Not as close as I'd have liked them to, but close enough. I snapped them both through the gap in the curtains. I couldn't hear what they were saying, but Gail was laughing, and Lycra Boy was looking down her cleavage like all his Christmases had come at once. I wondered what he'd say when Brendan Mackie caught up with him. Not a lot, most likely.

Come on, Gail. You haven't got all night. I hoped not, anyhow; I'd have to be off at seven myself, or lose the gig, and it was coming up to a quarter to already. What I really wanted was incontrovertible proof of the suspect's infidelities; something to confront Brendan with (and to earn that fee). Gail just sitting there wasn't enough; and there was no telling whether the evidence I had already gleaned would convince Brendan Mackie. I moved closer to the window, shifting the angle of the camera – and then a hand roughly the size and weight of a York ham descended on my shoulder, and a face the colour of a York ham pushed into mine, and a familiar voice rumbled up from out of the face and said: 'Bloody hell, it's Elvis.'

'Brendan!' My trained voice jumped an octave. 'Ah – how was the match?'

'We were robbed. Two-nil. Bloody referee.' He frowned a little, as if just beginning to take in the turned-up collar, the unfamiliar hairstyle, the digital mini-camera in my hand. 'Ay up,' he said, moving his hand to my throat. 'What's going on here?'

I began to explain. I'd hardly started, though, when Gail came running out of the house with a newspaper over her head and Lycra Boy in tow. 'It's him!' she said shrilly. 'It's that bloody perv from the gym!'

Now was the time for some rapid thinking. 'Harry Stone,' I said, waving my card. 'Private investigator.'

'Private what?' said Brendan, Gail and Lycra Boy in unison.

Gail was looking at my card.

'Harry Stone,' she read aloud, 'Private investigator, all cases considered, marital disputes a speciality. Bren?' She turned to her husband with eyes like lasers. 'What the bloody hell's going on here?'

Brendan Mackie looked shifty. His hand left my throat, and my cowboy boots went back to ground level, where they belonged.

'Anyroad, this isn't even a proper card,' continued Gail in a shrill voice. 'It's just a computer print, with the stamp drawn on in Biro.'

'He were watching us,' added Lycra Boy, surprising me (I'd have thought he'd have legged it fast, once he saw his number was up). 'Taking pictures of our Gail and the lasses in the gym.'

'You *what*?' Ouch. This wasn't going quite the way I'd planned it. *Our Gail.* Could it be that I had overlooked some detail? Too late I remembered Lily saying something about a gay brother who worked at the Body In Question. Glancing back at Lycra Boy, with his stripey blond hair and suspiciously even tan, I could see – too late – the family resemblance.

Brendan grabbed my collar again. 'You little pervert!'

Too late, I tried to pocket the camera. But Brendan was too fast for me; in a second he was going through the images on screen, his face looking more like raw ham than ever. I suppose I should have run for it. But it would have been ignoble and unworthy – of me, of Harry Stone, and most of all, of Elvis.

So what *would* Elvis have done? Burst into song, most likely, or sucker-punched Brendan in the mouth before he had time to react. For myself, I didn't fancy either alternative, and anyway, I bet even the King of Rock 'n' Roll might have had some difficulty getting out of *that* particular quandary, especially if he was dangling twelve inches off the ground at the end of Brendan Mackie's arm.

'It were an undercover job,' I said, in a strangled voice.

'Under*wear*, more like, you perv,' said Gail.

'Look, Brendan, I don't even *fancy* your Gail—'

'What?' His face darkened. 'Are you saying my wife's ugly?'

'No! I'm sorry!'

'You will be,' said Brendan, raising his fist.

'Not me face,' I protested, 'I got a gig on tonight …'

For a second his blurry fist obscured all my vision, like some gigantic meteor about to hit the earth. I closed my eyes, thinking *this is it, I'll never work the clubs again unless they take Elephant Man acts,* and then came a quiet and familiar voice from out of the shadows, and everything stopped.

It was Lily, of course. She must have been watching from up the road, and run across when she saw what was happening. She took Brendan firmly by the arm, and he released his grip. Like I said, she's a big girl.

'Now then,' said Lil. 'What's the matter?'

Brendan repeated the garbled tale. Gail and Lycra Boy corroborated it. I stood by, feeling like a prat.

'And you thought he was after *Gail*?' said Lil, when he'd finished.

'Well, yeh,' said Lycra Boy. 'I mean, who else?'

Lily just looked at him. After a moment or two, so did Gail.

'You don't mean—'

Lil nodded. 'You didn't *know*?'

They were all looking at me now. Even Brendan had a smile on his face. 'Well, come to think of it …'

'*Hang on!*' I said.

I was beginning to get the gist now, and I didn't like it much. 'I'm bloody straight, me. Straight as a die. Honest to God—' Then Lily gave me one of her stares, and I shut up. It wasn't easy, though; and from the looks on their faces I was sure the news would be all over the village by next week. Dammit. That really would put a crimp on my gig at the Rat – you can practically *smell* the testosterone in that place. An Elvis act – a *short* Elvis act – was hard enough – but a *queer* Elvis act would be downright suicidal.

'Bugger,' I said.

Lycra Boy gave me a sympathetic look. ''S all right, man,' he said. 'I were in denial for years before I came out.'

'Aye, he were dead shy,' said Gail. She was smiling now. Even Brendan was smiling, which was the only good news as far as I was concerned, and his face was now looking more like cooked ham rather than raw. 'You know, there's places you can go. Clubs and that. I bet yer act'd go down a bomb at the Pink Panther. And you'd get to *meet* people –' she patted my arm – ''stead of hanging around the B 'n Q.'

Well, that was that. Words failed me. I gave Lily a reproachful glance, but she was looking the other way. She might have saved my life, I thought bitterly, but what price my self-respect?

So that was the end of the Brendan Mackie case. Well, not quite; there was an unexpected silver lining to the whole fiasco, which paid both for my expenses, and to some extent, re-established my credibility. You see, Gail was right about those clubs. Top billing at the Pink Panther on a Friday night – hundred quid a gig, plus tips and drinks – and a rave review in the local press: *Jim Santana, the loudest, proudest Elvis act in the business.* That's what the *Morning Post* said, and I've had it printed onto my calling cards. Overnight, I've become a kind of celebrity. Suddenly everyone wants to book my act, and Bernie at the Lord Nelson's offered to reinstate me at twice my usual rate.

Still, as I told Lily the other night at the Cape Cod, this means that now I'll have to work even harder to keep Harry Stone in the shadows. 'I'm not in it for the money, Lil,' I said. 'Fame's a fickle friend, as Elvis knew, and I'll never let those bright lights seduce me. The stage may be my secret passion, but detective work's my *life*.'

Lily nodded awkwardly, without meeting my gaze. I have to say I might have been a bit harsh with her recently, what with the comments I'd been getting from Brendan Mackie and the blokes down the pub. In fact it was the first time I'd been in the Cod since the Mackie affair, and I could tell that Lily was worried that her contribution to the fiasco might have soured our special relationship. Her hands were shaking slightly as she checked the temperature of the deep-fat fryer, and there was a flush on her cheeks that was more than just the heat. Seeing that, I felt something begin to thaw inside me. I can never stay mad with Lily for long, you know, and besides, it was Friday night, and that means fish for supper.

'So, what now?' she asked shyly, putting a haddock in to fry. The deep-fat fryer hissed and slurred as the fish hit the fat, and I felt my mouth begin to water. No one does fish like Lily does; and no one does chips like she does, either; skin on, hand-cut, and just the right size. Salt, vinegar, mushy peas and scraps, all wrapped in hot greasy paper and a copy of the *Daily Mail.*

It was just one small step away from perfection.

'Fishcake?' she said, looking at me.

Elvis would.

'Yeah, go on then.'

So I did.

'Being a working mum means for me existing in an eternal state of guilt. When I'm with my kids I worry about all the work I'm not doing, and when I'm at work I worry about all the mothering I'm not doing. The only comfort I have is knowing I'm not alone in my agony, but suffering along with every other woman in my position.'

Mariella Frostrup

Happy Mother's Daze

Kathy Lette

I had never seen myself as the mothering type. Hell, I'd make Medea look like good mother material. I only knew how to look after dogs. If I ever did procreate, the kid would be cocking its leg on trees within days. I just didn't like ankle-biters. How could you not dislike someone who can eat sweets all day without putting on any weight?

Besides, I already had five godchildren. And was expecting a sixth. No. I had absolutely no intention of dilating my cervix the customary three kilometres for the pleasure of spending the rest of my life in bathrooms applauding bowel movements.

When I hit thirty all my aged relatives began pestering me about when I was going to produce progeny. 'Why?' I demanded. Just because they were in their eighties didn't mean I kept going up and asking them when they were expecting to get their first incontinence pads, now did I?

But then I awoke one morning to a very peculiar ticking sound. Yep. The snooze alarm had gone off on my biological clock. 'So?' gay friends shrugged. 'Get a digital.'

But it was too late. The sonar echo was there in all my thoughts. It resonated from the depths – motherhood. How could I chicken out of my obligation to my eggs? I may have been thirty in human years, but in Childless Female Years that was about three hundred and thirty! Besides which, Engagement, Marriage, The First Baby ... weren't those the traditional greeting card hallmarks of life? Let's face it, I was already programmed to the baby's schedule – up all night, drinking.

Taken hostage by my hormones, I suddenly found myself with an uncontrollable craving for kids. I spent hours envisaging my future *Kinder* frolicking at my perfectly pedicured feet. Hell, my family was going to make the Waltons look depressed. It was time to find a sperm happy to get egg all over its face. Yep, I was about to enter a new phase in my life ... The phase where you're in and out of stirrups more often than National bloody Velvet.

But no matter how bad the birth, it's a doddle compared with what follows. A baby resembles the most selfish, demanding lover you've ever had. Always hungry, but won't eat what you cook. Always tired, yet won't sleep. Tossing things all over the house, yet never picking up after himself. Throwing tantrums, yet never saying he's sorry. And possessive! A baby is jealous of other people coming anywhere near you. He hates you being on the phone. He won't even let you go to the loo on your own. All day long he just sits around in his vest, waiting to be amused. Which is difficult, as you no longer have a social life. (The baby got hold of your Filofax and dates May–June.) That's the other thing nobody had warned me about. The boredom. Sometimes I was so bored doing Creative Things With Play-Doh that I could actually see my plants engaging in photosynthesis. Once, I grew a yeast infection – for a change of pace.

You'll know you're definitely a few nappies short of a packet of Pampers when you find yourself sitting in the playpen with the baby sitting out of it, giving you one of those disappointed 'Hey, I gave you the best year of my life!' looks.

Is it any wonder that since my children were born I've only used one word with more than two syllables in it? The word was 'tranquilliser', because that's what I needed ... See Mother Run! See Mother Talking to Herself! See Mother Unable to Get the Child-proof Lid off the Valium Bottle!

For years I clung to the illusion that motherhood would improve once they hit puberty. But with a fifteen- and a twelve-year-old, I'm still bored and exhausted. But also derided for every outfit and opinion. 'Oh, Mum.

You're just sooooooo embarrassing.' Gee, if only I were young enough to know everything. I'm not allowed to sing, dance, laugh or wear short skirts.

Hell, having a teenager daughter is like living with the Taliban.

The world is groaning beneath weighty statues of mouldy old soldiers and long-forgotten politicians. What I want to see are statues to 'The Unknown Soldier – a Mother of Five Teenagers'. I want an inscription which reads 'A toddler AND a day job'. I mean, imagine a job-description of motherhood – Hours: constant. Time off: zilch. All food and entertainment supplied by you. Must be good at athletics, home repairs and making mince interesting. No sick pay, no holiday pay, hell, no pay! Would you take this job?

And yet we do. Although occasionally tempted to push my kids back into the condom-vending machine for a refund, like all mums I love my progeny with a primal passion. Maybe it has something to do with the way my son comes home from school and throws his arms around my neck, as passionate as Rhett Butler. Or the way your heart flops like a pole-vaulter into a mattress, as dreams flicker across your daughter's face, soft as sunlight. Or kissing those ivory eyelids, the caramel-coloured lashes so long you could positively hike through them. The way you finally appreciate your own wonderful mother. The immunisation children give you against loneliness. And pretension – kids have the most finely tuned crap antennas. The way babies wear their four hair strands combed horizontally over their heads in a fashion favoured by gerontophile news-readers. The way toddlers babble at you, talking in exclamation marks, punctuated with peals of silver laughter. The way they turn even hardened cynics sentimental. (Who could have predicted you'd become the mother version of Cecil B. DeMille, videoing every nano-second of your kids' lives for the archives – then immediately viewing the footage. 'Brings back memories, doesn't it?' you whimper, teary-eyed, to your husband.) The way you feel a massive joy squeeze into your bone marrow whenever they tell you they love you. The fact that it is the greatest love affair you'll ever have. For life. Unconditional.

Although kids, if you're reading this, there are a few conditions:

1) Please stop disappearing up the stairs with the maths tutor between your teeth; and
2) Just remember that perfect mothers only exist in American sitcoms.

'Never wear dark colours when your children have colds unless you want to look like you've been attacked by an army of snails!'

Melanie Sykes

Night Out

Caitlin Davies

Mum says I should get out more; I'm supposed to say yes to every invitation I get. That way I'll meet a nice man, have a nice baby, and start things all over again. As if.

But I did say yes to the hen night and I did spend ages looking for a present. I looked in the shops and on the Internet and in my sister-in-law's catalogues. I looked at chocolate-filled willies and willy bath plugs and bras made from sweets. I looked at fur handcuffs, an inflatable ball and chain, L-signs and leather whips. In the end I just bought a bottle of champagne. That was what people probably did on hen nights, I thought, get drunk. Not that I'd ever had one myself.

I had the bottle all ready in a bag, right in the middle of the landing, so I wouldn't forget it when the babysitter arrived.

Yvonne was the best babysitter I'd had. First there had been the girl from next door who wore black shoes as high as stilts. She was good, until her boyfriend dumped her and I came back to find she had put Jessie to bed naked on a winter's night and she herself was lying inert on the living-room floor, in a totally darkened room. She was thinking of spells, she said, spells to get her boyfriend back. I didn't go out for a long time after that.

Then there was the girl from downstairs with the pin in her nose, and again it was a boyfriend that caused the trouble, because he came round and emptied my fridge. Yvonne in comparison was an angel. She said it was due to the fact she had four children herself. I couldn't believe she had four children at her age, although I was too embarrassed to ask what her age was, or to ask for references.

'Right, I'm off,' I told her soon after she'd arrived. 'Jessie needs to be in bed *and asleep* by eight. She can have a bath if she wants. She can have anything *healthy* like an apple or … or … or anything healthy. Maybe some toast. But *definitely not* the cake in the fridge because that's for ….'

Yvonne stood patiently on the landing, waiting. I still hadn't let her in. Then she began to unweave a red and green scarf decorated with riding Santas from around her neck, slowly and with great concentration as if she were about to reveal something unexpected and fabulous underneath.

'Right, I'm off,' I said, distracted by the scarf and by

wondering what was underneath. Last time it had been a sweatshirt with a Playboy bunny. 'You've got my mobile number. I'll ring you just before I'm home. Jessie's pyjamas are on the radiator upstairs. Right …' I took a look around the room. I felt there was something I had left undone. Jessie had been sick last week; perhaps I shouldn't go.

'Mum!' Jessie shouted from upstairs.

'Yvonne's here. Come down.'

I looked up the stairs to see Jessie had squeezed her face between the banisters, right between the wooden rails so she looked like a portrait in a frame. Then she wailed, 'Don't go, Mum …'

'Oh God,' I muttered, and I thought about what my own mum said. 'She blackmails you that child.' But Jessie was only four; she couldn't be that calculating.

'I think I've got a fever, Mum,' she said, still with her face between the banisters.

'Really?' I took two steps up and I reached out my arm and felt her forehead with my hand, and it was as cool and uncrumpled as a new sheet.

Soho was busy that evening and on the streets people walked like fireworks. The buildings on Old Compton Street were brightly coloured even in the dark and no one seemed to have any children with them. As I walked I swung the bag with the champagne. I could see the top of the Post Office Tower: it used to be so tall when I was a child and now it looked like a leftover piece of Dalek. Then I remembered I hadn't given Yvonne the address, I hadn't said where I was going. Perhaps Jessie's dad would call and she would say I had gone out and she didn't know where, and then he would see his chance and come round and get her.

I was thinking about turning into Greek Street. It looked nice with its old-fashioned streetlights, its red-brick buildings the colour of veins. I could see café signs and awnings of cloth concertinas, doorways with brass letterboxes and plants spilling from window boxes like moss. Then my mobile rang. 'Hello?'

'Hi, Mum.' Jessie gave a deep sigh.

'Are you OK?' I asked, alarmed.

'Yes, but I really am missing you, Mum …'

'And I miss you too. But I'm out and I'll be back soon. OK?' I stuffed the phone back in my pocket. I had made it this far. And it was exciting to be out, to be out just before Christmas when the air felt flurried and crisp. All around me people were heading out for the night, perfume so freshly applied that I smelt a burst with each person that passed. This was another world and I was in it, I was walking as quickly as everyone else, I had somewhere to go. I put my hand in my coat pocket and found a small chocolate wrapped in foil. I must have taken it off Jessie but I couldn't remember when. As I walked through

Soho, I swung my bag of champagne and I ate the chocolate and I licked the sweetness around my tongue.

'Could you help me to cross?'

I looked around, to see who was speaking, to see if they were speaking to me. On the kerb was a woman about my mother's age and her head was darting from left to right, watching the cars, searching for a safe gap in which to cross.

'Of course,' I said, smiling. I had the feeling the woman had been standing there for some time. Even as we stood there, the pavement filled up twice with people and then cleared again. The woman could have been here for hours, waiting for someone to help.

She put out her left elbow and I linked it with mine and, slowly, a little unsteadily, we made our way across the road. It felt comforting, walking arm in arm. I felt strong and helpful; the woman was so much shorter, so much older than me.

'There you go,' I said, as we reached the other side.

'Where's Goose Lane?' said the woman, her arm still lightly in mine.

'Where?' People were pushing past us. A man tottered on high heels; three women spoke in Italian, laughing.

'Goose Lane. Is it right, down there? Do you know?' The woman spoke quietly, as if not wanting to be overheard.

A man with a briefcase barged past me and I moved further onto the pavement, bringing the elderly woman with me. In front of us a group of women, with sparkly pointed hats on, were walking, arm in arm, heels clackety-clacking on the pavement.

'Sorry, I've no idea.'

The woman pulled me close then as a fire engine passed, siren screaming, startling both of us. And I thought, what if there's a fire at home and Jessie needs help? A fire at home while I was walking through Soho with a bag of champagne, on my way to a hen night. Had I changed the batteries in the smoke alarm?

'Goose Lane, do you know where it is?' asked the woman.

'Are you lost?'

'Oh no,' the woman smiled, and I looked at her face properly now. It was soft and powdery and her lips were painted a subtle pink. She knew how to wear make-up; she had not slapped it on in the dark. It was carefully applied so that a dusting of blue on the lids brought out the colour of her eyes. And I could see her earrings, big golden hoops that reminded me of a pair my mother had once had, only these were so shiny it was as if they had just been taken, unused, out of a box.

'No, I'm not lost exactly, just a little forgetful,' the woman laughed.

I smiled. We would all get forgetful. I would. I

would especially, because it ran in my genes, because my mother was forgetful. And I wondered, fleetingly, who helped my mother when she wanted to cross the road and if she had got to the stage when she needed help to cross a road and, if she had, whether or not she would ask anyone to help. Probably not, I thought. But if she refused to move nearer to me, then what could I do about it?

'Goose Lane?' I queried. 'Is it off this road?'

'Oh yes. It's either the first right or the first left.' The woman pulled at something round her neck and I saw it was a piece of fur and that it still had the head of a small ferret-like creature attached. The woman eased the fur down across the collar of her coat and I had the feeling then that she belonged to a different age, a different class. Perhaps she was going to the theatre, perhaps dinner with a gentleman friend at a private members' club, perhaps she would begin her evening with a Martini with a cherry on top.

'Shall we find out?' I asked. If you couldn't stop and help someone in life, then what was the point? I looked up and saw we were passing a billboard advertising a play, a giant *Mamma Mia!* sign, and I was not sure if the woman in the picture wearing the wedding dress was screaming or laughing.

The woman smiled and gave my arm a little squeeze. We walked on companionably and stopped at the next crossroad. I read out the street names, to show her there was no Goose Lane.

'Perhaps the next one?' she suggested. 'Or we could go this way.'

We walked on and turned into another road.

'What is it you're looking for?' I asked. 'I mean, is it a restaurant or something?'

'It is where I live,' the woman said, and she looked me directly in the eye. And I don't know why but I looked down then and I saw her shoes. Only they were not really shoes, they were remains of shoes. The leather on the sides was there, but there was nothing at the front, and on the top only some thin grey shoelaces with knots so tight they would never be undone.

People hurried all round us, coming out of buildings, waiting in lines before the glass doors of bars, hanging out of second-floor windows, crossing roads. And still I looked at her shoes.

'Would you mind,' she said, 'if we tried a little further?'

'No, no, of course,' I said hurriedly, too hurriedly because of her shoes. The air was bitter now, but I didn't want to look down in case her toes were purple. People were still pushing past us and it was so noisy that it took me a moment to realise my mobile was ringing.

'Hello?'

Jessie gave a big sigh. 'Hello, Mum. Can you come home as quickly as possible?'

'Why?'

'Because I miss you so much, Mum.'

'Where's your babysitter?'

'What, Mum?'

'Is Yvonne there?'

'I think so.'

'You *think* so? You shouldn't be on the phone anyway, Jessie. It's …' I looked at the front of my phone. 'It's nearly nine! Why aren't you in bed? Does Yvonne *know* you're on the phone?'

'*Mum* …'

'Jessie! I've told you, I'm going to be back soon. OK? OK?' And I put the phone away with a little trembly feeling of guilt.

'It's near Joan's,' said the woman, and she peered up at me, her eyes wavery, like sea seen through a dirty porthole. She said it a little annoyed, as if my attention shouldn't be elsewhere.

'Your friend Joan?'

'The department store,' the woman said, and she looked even more annoyed as if it was exhausting having to remind me. 'I don't feel well,' she said, and she puffed air through her lips, rapidly, a couple of times.

'So you live nearby, near the department store?'

'Oh, I recognise this!' the woman said, and she quickened her pace. She led the way across another road and into an alleyway. It was dark, there were no streetlights, and there was an odd haze, like sun or smoke. For a moment we were alone, I couldn't see or hear any other people.

'Are you sure you recognise this?'

But the woman didn't reply. She was walking quickly now, tugging me after her down the alleyway that was cobbled underfoot. I looked around, at the blackened wall of an entrance to a kitchen, at a cat sitting on a doorstep nipping at itself, at a couple arguing in front of a doorway beside a doorman in a peaked cap who looked like he was pretending to be somewhere else. There was no sign of a department store, unless some years ago these buildings had been all part of one place, a time when things had been less crowded than they were today.

'Excuse me.' I stopped a man coming the other way. He wore a suit but his tie was loosened at the neck as if he had just left work. The man kept on walking. 'Excuse me!' I called, annoyed. 'Do you know where there's a department store around here? Called Joan's?'

The man looked at me and then at my companion.

'She's lost,' I said.

Beside me I felt the woman stiffen.

'She's a little lost and we need to find …'

The man gave a tight smile, skirted around us, and hurried on.

'Excuse me!' I called to another, older man, who was passing us now on the pavement. He quickly stepped onto the road and crossed to the other side. 'I'm sorry,' I said to the woman, loudly and pointedly, 'but no one wants to stop to help us.'

We walked on, turning right and then left. We walked past a bar whose windows were open onto the cold night and by the windows two men were sitting, both on their mobile phones. The air suddenly turned to specks of snow and the specks fell down on us like blossom. The woman's grasp was becoming heavy now; she was leaning on me, leaning into me, and I felt that if I let go she would perhaps collapse. I could smell dried parsley and tissue paper. I couldn't believe no one wanted to help us. How was an elderly woman to find her way home?

We set off again, stepping back into the road to avoid three enormous dustbins balanced outside a Chinese restaurant, and then back onto the pavement again. And I wondered what I was going to do, whether I was going to keep on walking through Soho all night with an elderly woman who was lost. I calculated how much I already owed the babysitter. I thought about pulling my arm away, sending the woman on her way, turning back and going to the hen night I was supposed to have been at an hour ago. In my left hand the bag with the champagne felt heavy. I pulled out my phone, thinking I would call my friends to say I was late, but there was no reception.

'Oh! This is it!' the woman said.

'It is?'

'Yes, this is certainly the way,' and she sped up again, pulling me with her. I couldn't work out if we were a long way from where we'd started, or if we had just been going round in an endless square.

'Shall I call the police?' I asked, but she didn't seem to have heard me. She was standing still now, one foot on the pavement and one foot on the road, and her neck was strained because she was staring up into the sky. I tried to shift my arm but she squeezed her fingers round my elbow until I could feel my own bone. I tried to move on, but she held me back.

'Look, I'm sorry, but I've got to—'

'Oh! *Where* is it?' the woman said, and she wailed like a child whose toy has unfairly been taken away.

So I took out my phone and dialled 999.

'Hi, um, I don't know if it's OK ...'

'Fire, police or ambulance?'

'Police, I suppose. It's just that ...'

'Hello?'

'Hi. Sorry. I'm not sure whether I should, well, it's just that I'm with this woman here, in Soho, and she's elderly and lost and she's ...' I looked down again at the woman's shoes.

'Where are you?'

I frowned. I had no idea where I was. I looked up

and around, desperately searching for a street name. 'Duck Lane. Duck Lane is just on the right.'

As I put the phone back in my pocket the woman tugged me, she wanted to move on. But I had just told the police where we were, I couldn't move now.

'Wait!' I said as she pulled me. 'Just wait here a minute, I'm just trying to get some help.'

Then I saw a police officer heading down the street towards us.

'Oh, thank God,' I said. For the first time in my life I really wanted to see a policeman, even if he did look so young. 'Look, he'll—'

'Get off me!' the woman snapped.

'What?' I turned to look at her, confused. Perhaps I had accidentally stepped on her foot. Perhaps she was speaking to someone else.

'GET OFF ME!'

I looked down at her. Her cheeks were red where a few minutes ago they had been powdery and her lips were clenched.

'JUST GET OFF ME!' she screamed again, and the words came out all jagged as if she were fighting something terrible, as if that something terrible was me. But I couldn't get off her because she still held onto me. Then with one hand she still held onto me, but with the other hand she slapped me on the shoulder.

It was not a hard slap, but still I was surprised and I

tried to pull myself away. Then she slapped me harder, her hand against my neck, slapping like a flip-flop on a pavement. Again I tried to draw back, to keep my face away, but she stood up tall on her tiptoes, as tall as she could make herself, and she slapped my cheeks with a sharp crack.

And still holding on and still slapping me, she dragged me right into the road. I could feel the impact of the slaps; my skin fizzed in the cold. But I felt as if I was tied up; I couldn't hit her back.

A taxi screeched and the driver swore, 'What the fuck!' and made a big display of driving round us. A group of people on the kerb stopped to watch; they looked as if they were coming from the theatre, for two of the women had capes on and shiny little handbags. They were staring at me, their expressions disapproving. One of the men made as if to cross the road towards us, but two companions held him back.

'WHAT ARE YOU DOING TO ME!' the woman screamed and she flayed her fingers in the air.

'But I was *helping* you,' I said, and I tugged my arm, pulling to get it out of hers, to show the people watching that she was the one who was hanging onto me.

Then suddenly she released me and I stumbled while she went flying off down the middle of the road, the sides of her broken shoes flapping.

'Everything OK?' the policeman said. He didn't look

very pleased. He looked as if he were going to start by treating me politely and then ask me to accompany him to the station. I felt tears prick at the back of my eyes and I squeezed them shut. The woman had disappeared; I couldn't see where she had gone. Then I pulled out my ringing phone.

'Mum,' sighed Jessie. 'I just want to say, you have a lovely evening because you deserve to go out and have some fun. And Mum? This chocolate cake is really delicious.'

Motherhood

Santa Montefiore

Last night, our three-year-old son Sasha woke up again in the middle of the night. My sleep is very shallow these days; all the children need to do is whimper and I'll be up there by their beds, stroking their brows, whispering words of reassurance, frightening the monsters out of the shadows. I need my sleep. A bad night means I can barely concentrate on the novel I'm writing. It means another wasted day feeling groggy, filling up on tea, raiding the biscuit tin, promising myself that tomorrow I'll get down to it, write a chapter, go on a diet. Never once do I blame my child, even though my own mother tells me I'm spoiling him and that I should leave him to cry himself back to sleep. Motherhood is a miraculous thing; I can love these two people more than I love myself. In those dead hours before dawn breaks, when I can barely keep my eyes open, I am able to muster up the strength to caress them back to sleep. My love for them is so strong, I'd fight those monsters with my bare hands if I had to and never once do I begrudge them for it.

Before I became a mother my life was all about me. Through school and university and various jobs in London, my thoughts concentrated entirely on my own desires and needs. Then I became a wife and it was all about us. We'd lie in on a Sunday, have lunch in a restaurant with friends, take a walk around The Serpentine, have tea in a café. We'd go to the cinema, stay out late, go to Paris for the weekend. We could be spontaneous. I looked back on my childhood with nostalgia, because I grew up on a farm and in my memory the days were always sunny and there were always hay bales to jump on and woods to build camps in. Yet, I never considered my parents. They were there, giving everything so that we could have the best life has to offer; but I never appreciated their sacrifice or the love that lay behind it, until I became a mother.

Our daughter, Lily, was born in 2001. My first novel was due out the same month. I celebrated my book launch with an enormous belly, and planned to tour France and Germany a month after giving birth to promote it. As far as I was concerned, my life really didn't have to change very much. After all, writing is a job one can do at home and I'd have a maternity nurse to look after her while I was away.

However, the moment that little girl came into the world, my own small world shifted with an enormous jerk. Suddenly, nothing was more important than her. The love I felt was something I could never have imagined before. Like describing a painting to a blind person with no experience of colour, a mother's love for her child is impossible to explain. I held her against me, this little miracle of life, and knew that I'd never go to France and Germany and I really didn't care if I never wrote another book again. My husband and I gazed upon her for hours, celebrating each twitch, marvelling at the perfection of Nature and the existence of a power far greater than us. I was humbled. Together we had brought her into the world, but she had come from Heaven.

With the birth I shed a skin, leaving my emotions exposed and vulnerable. If I get sick, I can cope. I believe I have an inner strength and philosophy that would enable me to face whatever life deals me. However, if my child gets sick I'm powerless, hopeless and in despair. I'll endure anything in the place of my child because the anguish of watching my child suffer would be far greater than any physical pain. I remember when I was eighteen, my mother had a terrible skiing accident where she was hit by an enormous avalanche and thrown hundreds of feet down a cliff face. She broke pretty much everything and had to be dug out and resuscitated. Yet, in spite of having to endure countless operations, give up her favourite sport, which she had done with great skill and beauty, and facing an uncertain future, she has always thanked God it happened to her and not one of her children. I understand her now.

Like other mothers I can't read horror stories about children in the press. They cut me to the quick. I empathise too much, identify too much, and worry even more about my own children. I grew up with such freedom. In the summer, my brother, sister and I would wander up the drive, which is about a quarter of a mile long, and play on the mountains of corn in our pyjamas, without a care in the world. My mother never worried about paedophiles stalking the country lanes. Yet, when I'm there with my own children, I can barely let them wander the gardens on their own, even though my parents' house is miles from anywhere. I certainly wouldn't let them walk up the drive on their own. I look upon other people's children differently too, with far more compassion, and I don't pull irritated faces at the mother of the screaming child on the plane, because I have been there too and know how she feels.

Becoming a mother automatically made me a member of a club I never knew existed before. Suddenly I had something in common with parents all over the globe, from every walk of life. I discovered that most taxi drivers are parents, like me fiercely proud of their children, and chatting about them is mutually interesting.

However, one can only indulge in such talk to other members of the club, for rabbiting on about one's children to those outside the club is as boring as discussing sport with people who don't play.

Sasha was born with my third novel in 2003. My doubts about loving another child as much as Lily were dispelled the moment I held him. My family was now complete: a girl and a boy. I have two arms, one for each, and a heart big enough for both. I learned that it is possible to love two children in different ways, each child requiring something different from me, touching me in different ways, yet equally special. I am constantly surprised by them and always aware of the example I'm setting, because like teaching a child to hold a knife and fork, children have to learn to love. It's a constant pleasure to watch them grow and develop. I love to watch them playing happily together. It upsets me so much when they fight, as it used to upset my mother. Don't they know that family is everything?

Watching Lily and Sasha grow has made me aware of how fragile children are. It is our responsibility and duty to encourage them and praise them, while at the same time giving them security with boundaries that teach them the difference between right and wrong. Their spirits are in our hands and we have the power to crush them or make them grow. Yet, I believe there is a part of them, at their very core, that we cannot reach. Children survive in spite of their parents because of this inaccessible place; their soul – the part I believe doesn't come from us.

Looking back on my own childhood I was given a great deal of freedom. My father has always maintained that one cannot teach wisdom. One can teach knowledge, but wisdom has to be learned through experience. With this in mind, a child needs to be set free to make mistakes so that he may grow. There have been many times in my life when I have gone against advice, believing I know what is best for me, only to find I am wrong. However, no experience is wasted. We are all here to evolve spiritually and I have learned many important lessons with each experience. Yet, I gasp in horror at the thought of my own children making the same blunders I have made. I want to protect them from life, cocoon them and keep them safe. Yet, I cannot.

My parents sent me to boarding school at the age of eight. I adored every minute of it. Riding out over the hills before breakfast during the summer term. Climbing the cedar tree and building camps in the avenue of chestnut trees called 'Chestnut Village'. Playing 'chain he' on the lawn, leaping over the long evening shadows before the bell summoning us to bed, eating toffee apples on bonfire night and dressing up for the old headmistress's birthday party. I only cried occasionally, during that long journey back to school in the dark and drizzle, then watching my parents' headlights disappear up the drive from my dorm window. But it didn't last long and soon I was swallowed up into the magical spirit of the place, surrounded by friends, noise and laughter.

When I was eighteen I spent a year in Argentina. It was too expensive to telephone so I wrote to my parents weekly. I didn't miss home. I fell in love with the country, rode horses, learned Spanish, experienced a sense of freedom I had never had – being fresh out of boarding school – and had a rocky but exciting romance with a polo player. I barely had time to think about my mother, but all the time in the world to think about myself.

It was only when I grew up that my mother told me how she used to cry all the way home in the car after leaving me at boarding school. How she missed me. She wrote to me every day and sent me parcels. She drove the hour and a quarter just to deliver my birthday cake and never missed a school concert, carol service, netball match or play. While I was thinking only of myself, my mother's days revolved around her children as mine do now. It must have been hard for my parents to watch me fly off to the other side of the world. Hard for them to me let go. I didn't consider their feelings. It is only now that I am a mother that I understand them and what they have been through loving us.

I am grateful for the golden childhood they gave me. For always being there with open arms we could run into. I never once doubted their affection. The fact that I never considered it is testament to their consistent, unconditional love. It was always there, like a soft and solid rug beneath my feet. If one grows wise through experience, then my childhood experience has taught me a great deal as I fumble along the path of motherhood. My parents loved me enough to let me go. They would have far preferred to keep me by their side, to watch over me and protect me from the mistakes I would inevitably make. Yet, they set me free. As Kahlil Gibran writes in *The Prophet*: 'Love possesses not nor would it be possessed'.

I don't think we will send our children to boarding school at eight, but we will certainly send them at twelve and thirteen. Right now I can't imagine them growing up. Being so small they are totally supervised. But grow up they will and my biggest challenge will be in letting them go. I will have to let them run wild in the woods and on the farm. All I can do is give them the right tools in order for them to carve out their own lives. We brought them into the world, but we don't own them. I think one of the hardest parts of being a mother is stepping back.

I continue to write a book a year. I've written seven. My office leads directly out into the garden, so my children wander in and out and I never close the door. I don't want them to ever feel they can't come in for a hug or a chat. Besides, they inspire me. Loving them has given my life another dimension. They have taught me that nothing is more important than the people I love. We can lose everything and survive, but I pray we don't lose each other.

I understand my parents now. I know the kind of love that inhales joy and fear in a single breath. I know what it is like to put others first because they matter far more than me. I know the promise these young lives hold in their small hands, but it is up to them how they use it, and that for me will be the biggest challenge of all.

'I was about 17 studying for my A-levels and had a vacation job during the Christmas holidays. I stayed out all night at a party and arrived home, in all my finery, at about 8.30 am.

"Where do you think you're going?" said my mum. "To bed," I mumbled. "Oh no, you're not. You have a job to go to and you're not letting them down."

She unceremoniously stripped me of my party gear, pulled on some work clothes and pushed me out of the door. A dramatic lesson in social responsibility.'

Dr Miriam Stoppard

At the Captain's Table

Gervase Phinn

Mrs de la Mare sat up stiffly on the sun lounger and surveyed the vast and empty ocean, her pale eyes hidden behind fashionable horn-rimmed sunglasses. Everything about her was expensive: the tailored navy linen trousers, the designer cream top, the delicate daytime pearls, the flawless make-up. Her small, down-turned mouth, like that of a peevish child, twitched involuntarily. The cruise had been a sad disappointment. She gave a small wearisome sigh, examined her perfectly manicured nails and reflected on the previous cruise. Standards, she thought, had certainly fallen.

It had been five years ago, just after her husband had died, that she had last been on a cruise ship. At Southampton she had boarded the *Empress Elizabeth* ('the very latest in world-class liners, elegance personified, stylish in design and sophisticated in atmosphere' – so the glossy brochure had assured her) and spent two rather cold, but not entirely unpleasant, weeks visiting the Norwegian fjords. Hubert, her late husband, had invested prudently and left her very well provided for and, a month after the funeral, she had bought a new wardrobe of clothes (with accessories) and booked a state room (with double balcony and bath) to 'discover the delights of spectacular Norway'. Of course, it had certainly not been all plain sailing, for Mrs de la Mare always found something not to her liking. As she had explained to her sister, Marcia, on her return, she had refused to lower her standards; only the best was good enough. The highlight of the cruise for her had not been the spectacular fjords, but when the captain had invited her to dine at his table. 'Such a charming man,' she had told Marcia, 'with beautiful table manners and most interesting conversation. We had so much in common.' It was her sister who had persuaded Mrs de la Mare to come on this cruise.

'Of course, Michael and I would love you to come with us to Vance for the summer, darling,' she had said, 'but you know how unbearable you found the heat the last time and then there were the mosquitoes which you found so irritating. And the French are not your favourite people, now, are they? A cruise would suit you down to the ground. You'll be the life and soul of the party, the talk of the captain's table.'

Reluctantly Mrs de la Mare had booked the cruise, but she knew, as soon as she saw her fellow passengers boarding the ship, that it had been a mistake. She noted, with a sinking heart and a scornful expression, the throng of people in the reception lounge: elderly couples, overweight women in tight jeans, men in shorts and trainers, and children – some in pushchairs. She predicted that she would not find this cruise to her liking at all. Even the sultry heat and the irritating mosquitoes in Vance, she thought, would have been an improvement on this.

Things were not at all satisfactory from the very beginning of the cruise. For a start the cabin seemed so much smaller. There were fewer drawers in the bedside cabinet, the wardrobe space was cramped and there wasn't enough room to swing a cat in the bathroom. Then there was her steward. It had taken him an age to deliver her cases to the cabin and then she was obliged to unpack herself. He was far less attentive and so much slower with her laundry and her early morning tea, that she had had to have a word with him. Of course, being foreign, he understood very little and just smiled and nodded. She thought of the last cruise when she merely had to press a button and the steward arrived in seconds, in pristine purple uniform and white gloves – nothing had been too much trouble for him.

Then there were the dining arrangements. She had been put on a corner table in the restaurant, with a group of people with whom she had nothing in common. There was a neurotic primary school headteacher and her dreary husband; a self-opinionated and jumped-up retired bank manager and his mousy little wife; and a garrulous old woman who, judging from her lack of any dress sense, dubious table manners and strong regional accent, had clearly got some sort of special offer to enable her to afford such a holiday. Things had certainly changed and not for the better. Such was her dissatisfaction with her table companions, that Mrs de la Mare had decided to dine alone in her cabin for the last three evenings.

What niggled Mrs de la Mare most, however, was that it was nearing the end of the cruise and the captain had not yet invited her to sit at his table. It was the custom for the captain to 'request the pleasure' of certain special passengers to dine with him one evening during the cruise, and on the previous sea-going excursion to the Norwegian fjords she had taken her place on the captain's table with the great and the good. A card, edged in gold, had been left in her cabin, inviting herself, and a select few of her fellow passengers, to join the captain for dinner. So far, on this cruise, no card had been delivered. She had watched with growing irritation, as the chosen ones enjoyed their dinner at the top table with the master and senior officers, while she had to sit and listen to the whingeing of the headteacher; interminable accounts about pensions and investments from the retired bank manager; and tiresome family sagas from the elderly woman. She was so annoyed and disinterested that she never paid the slightest attention to whatever any of them said. Mrs de la Mare had, of course, pointed out to the purser the captain's omission, adding that she wasn't just anybody – she was, after all, on A Deck, in an outside state room with double balcony and bath. As such, she would hope she was one of the rather more special and valued passengers on the ship. Perhaps the captain wasn't aware that she was aboard and ought to be acquainted of the fact. The purser, a small man with a shiny bald head, had smiled and told her politely that everyone on the ship was special but he would mention her presence to the captain.

Then there was the on-board entertainment. Mrs de la Mare would be the *first* to admit that she was no expert on classical music, but the concert pianist left a lot to be desired. She was, however, something of an *aficionado* of classical pianoforte music and, even if she said so herself, knew a great deal more than most. She had merely mentioned to him that, in her opinion, he needed a little more work on his Chopin. He had been so offensive, telling her that she might perhaps like to give everyone the benefit of her musical expertise and extensive knowledge, and demonstrate on the grand piano at the next recital. She had bristled with indignation and promptly reported him to the cruise director. He had explained to her that creative people do tend to be rather temperamental, but he told her politely that he would mention her complaint to the concert pianist.

Of course, she had had occasion to complain to the cruise director on a number of other occasions after this. She had shared her opinion with him that the port lecturer, that dusty old vicar who droned on and on like some dreadfully boring television programme which one couldn't turn off, would have been better occupied back at his church boring his congregation rather than lecturing on a cruise ship. No wonder the Church of England was in such a decline. She had also mentioned the 'international vocalist' (not that Mrs de la Mare had heard of her) who was far too loud and brash and not always on key. And then there was the 'side-splitting comedian' whose jokes were, to her mind, tasteless and far too *risqué*. And as for the special interest lecturer – some retired school inspector who wrote books about his experiences in the Yorkshire Dales – he was certainly of no special interest to her.

Mrs de la Mare gave another small sigh and closed her eyes momentarily. Yes, she thought, standards had unquestionably fallen.

'Hello.'

Mrs de la Mare opened her eyes and removed her sunglasses, to see the cheery face of the elderly woman from her dining table staring down at her. She gave a dry little smile. 'Good morning,' she replied. Her voice was deliberately cold and superior. The last thing she wanted was for the woman to join her.

'May I join you?' asked the woman, not waiting for a reply and sitting on the adjacent lounger. It creaked under the weight. Mrs de la Mare's companion was a heavy woman with a bay window of a bust, a round red moon of a face, large, inquisitive blue eyes and thick, wavy, tinted hair. She was wearing a garishly multi-coloured cotton smock – shapeless and timeless.

'I saw you sitting here all by yourself,' burbled the woman brightly and stretching out on the lounger, 'and thought you might like a bit of company.'

'How very kind of you,' replied Mrs de la Mare, her face as inexpressive as a blank wall. There was a quiet sarcasm in the tone of her reply.

'You looked such a lonely soul,' said the woman.

'I beg your pardon?' Mrs de la Mare drew a deep, exasperated breath, which was quite lost on her companion.

'Sitting here on your own.'

'I enjoy my own company,' Mrs de la Mare informed her tartly.

'And we haven't seen much of you,' said the woman cheerfully.

'We?' enquired Mrs de la Mare.

'On our table,' said the woman. 'You've not been down for dinner the last three evenings.'

'No,' replied Mrs de la Mare. 'I've dined in my cabin.'

'Everyone's been asking about you.'

'Really?' she asked wearily.

'We thought perhaps you were ill. Seasick or something. If truth be told, I'm a terrible sailor but, touch wood, I've been fine so far. Usually I only have to look at a wave and I go green at the gills. I get seasick gutting fish.' She laughed at her own witticism. 'I remember when me and my husband went to the Isle of Man on the ferry. Up and down was the sea like a fiddler's elbow. I was inside, heaving and splashing in the ladies' lavatory, and the sea was outside, heaving and splashing like there was no tomorrow. I thought I'd die.'

'Well, I don't get seasick,' Mrs de la Mare told her, replacing her sunglasses and wishing the woman would depart and leave her alone.

'My son, Robert, doesn't,' the woman told her. 'I don't know where he gets his liking for the sea from. My husband and I both like our feet on solid ground. Well, he *did*, my husband. As I say, he's passed on now. Had a heart attack tying up his boots. Robert asked if I wanted him to scatter his father's ashes at sea on his next trip, but I said no. My husband went queasy on a canal boat. He certainly wouldn't have wanted to end up floating in the North Sea on the currents of time.' The woman stretched back on the lounger and felt the warmth of the sun on her face. She sighed with contentment. 'Hasn't it been a lovely cruise?' she said.

Mrs de la Mare allowed herself a small smile. It was not a particularly pleasant smile. 'Hardly,' she murmured.

'Is it your first?' asked the woman.

'My first?' repeated Mrs de la Mare.

'Cruise? Is this your first cruise?'

'No, I have cruised before,' she told her.

'You'll be something of an old hand, then?'

Mrs de la Mare arched her finely pencilled eyebrows to their fullest extent. She didn't condescend to reply.

'It's *my* first cruise,' explained the woman, 'and, oh, how I've enjoyed it. It's been magical: the food, the entertainment, the interesting lectures, all the activities. It's been just perfect. Everything's so spotlessly clean and everybody's so friendly and helpful, aren't they? Nothing's too much trouble for them. I've not sat down once since I got on the boat.'

'Ship,' corrected Mrs de la Mare, with unyielding snobbishness. 'It's called a ship.'

The woman chuckled. 'I'm always calling it a boat. My Robert, he's forever telling me: "Mother," he says, "it's a ship, not a boat. A submarine's a boat, an ocean liner is a ship."'

'Quite the expert,' muttered Mrs de la Mare waspishly.

'It was my Robert who persuaded me to come on the cruise,' explained the woman. 'He loves the ocean. Always has done, ever since he was a little boy and he sailed his toy boat on the boating lake in Clifton Park. Never wanted to do anything else but go to sea. "You're going on a cruise, Mother," he says. He just wouldn't take no for an answer. He got some sort of special deal for me.'

Mrs de la Mare smiled and felt a tinge of triumph. Yes, she had thought as much – the woman was on some sort of special offer. She was probably in an inside cabin, single, in the bowels of the ship.

'He's been on and on at me since my husband died two years ago to come on a cruise, but I was a bit nervous,' continued the woman. 'As I said, I'm not the best sailor in the world and coming by myself was a bit of a worry, I don't mind saying. Frank, that was my husband, and me went everywhere together. It's strange going places without him. But everything's been just perfect. There's lots of us travelling by ourselves, and Richard and Emma, the entertainment officers – lovely young people, aren't they, and always cheerful – organise this "Travelling Alone Get-Together", every morning, where you can meet and get to know people. I've met some lovely people. You ought to come along. You'd like it.'

'I think not,' observed Mrs de la Mare, imagining the nightmare that the little get-together would be.

'There's so much to do,' continued the woman. 'Ballroom dancing, flower arranging, bridge, whist drives, bingo, quizzes, the casino, concerts and lectures, trips ashore, films, aerobics.'

'I *have* seen the itinerary,' Mrs de la Mare told her stiffly.

'I went for a facial treatment yesterday,' the woman told her, touching her round red face. 'Have you been?'

'No, I haven't,' replied Mrs de la Mare, rewarding her companion with an icy look.

'You ought to try it. I'm having a hot stone massage this afternoon, then a sauna and a manicure and then my hair done for the formal dinner tonight.'

'I couldn't trust anyone with my hair,' said Mrs de la Mare. 'Except, of course, my own hairdresser back home.'

'Barbara, in the beauty salon, is very good and what a character. Talk about facial treatment, I must have added a few more wrinkles after my session with her. I don't think I've ever laughed as much. She was telling me about what some of the passengers say to her. One woman asked her what time the ten o'clock – what do you call it – the ship that takes people ashore?'

'The tender,' Mrs de la Mare informed her. 'And that *is* a boat.'

'That's it. Well, this passenger asked her what time the ten o'clock tender was leaving. "Ten o' clock," Barbara told her. Don't some people ask some silly questions? "Oh," said the passenger, "and coming back, what end of the pier will it go from?" Then there was a man who asked her if there was a bus timetable in Venice. It's on islands, you know, is Venice.'

'Yes, I am aware of that,' said Mrs de la Mare. 'I have been to Venice – several times, actually.'

'She said you get all sorts on the cruise ships.'

Well, there's something we can agree upon, thought Mrs de la Mare, uncrossing her elegant ankles and making ready to escape.

'This cruise has been paradise,' sighed the woman. 'Holiday of a lifetime.'

'I'm afraid I can't share your enthusiasm,' Mrs de la Mare said. 'This being your first cruise, I am sure you are finding it most enjoyable. Now, if you will excuse me, I think it's time for my afternoon siesta.'

As she rose to her feet, her face suddenly broke into the practised smile which she had perfected for when someone of importance came into view. She had spotted the captain, a tall, distinguished-looking man with a broad and winning smile, striding towards her.

'There you are,' he called. 'I've been searching the ship for you.'

Mrs de la Mare felt a small glow of satisfaction in the knowledge that she would, after all, be dining that evening on the top table and on one of the two formal occasions, as well. The purser had indeed, she imagined, had a quiet word and the captain had come to apologise for his oversight. She rehearsed in her head what she would say. 'I should be delighted to join you.'

'Do excuse me,' said the captain, in the most solicitous of voices as he passed her by.

Then, much to her amazement, he leaned over her elderly companion and kissed her warmly on the cheek.

'Now, remember,' he said, 'cocktails at seven thirty and dinner at eight, and wear your best frock. You're on the captain's table tonight.'

'I will,' said the woman. She looked up at Mrs de la Mare, who was fixed to the spot, mouth open, eyes staring. 'This is my son, Robert,' said the woman. 'I'm sorry, I didn't catch *your* name.'

'Never flatter someone you don't like in front of your kids. As children, they are duty-bound to "out" you.'

Arabella Weir

Must I Paint You a Picture?

Mike Gayle

It's the summer of 1979. And I'm eight years old and it feels like it's been summer for ever. I've just come back from school and I'm playing on the pavement at the front of our house with a few of the neighbourhood kids. We're playing around with our bikes, kicking a football against the kerb – the usual kind of thing – when my friend Simon yells, 'Look at this!' When an eight-year-old yells this to a group of eight-year-olds, there's no beating about the bush – they look because one of the fundamental principles of being eight is that you know when something is so cool that it's worthy of the attention of your friends. Get it wrong and you'll never get to live it down. In an instant we drop everything and surround him. And he's right. It is 'look' worthy. Just in case we haven't seen it, he points at the floor near my next-door neighbour's hedge, but there's actually no missing the cause of the excitement. It's green and yellow with hairs all over its back. It's as long as a grown man's finger and as fat as a Winston Churchill cigar. A caterpillar. But unlike any caterpillar my friends and I have ever seen. It's huge in comparison to the creatures we have encountered.

'It's an alien,' says my friend Simon.

'No, it's not,' snaps my friend Kevin.

'So what is it, then?' replies Simon.

'It's a thing,' says Kevin. 'A thing.'

'The Thing', as it is dubbed, becomes the centre of attraction in our small cul-de-sac. As more kids come round to view The Thing, adults stop by to look too. Soon there are upwards of fifteen people crowded around The Thing, staring in wonder. Someone suggests that we call the local news and see if they want to take pictures of The Thing. In an instant my head is full of pictures of reporters with microphones, asking us to recall how we came across the creature huddled on the tarmac by my feet.

Mum (who had been cooking dinner for that evening) eventually noticed the commotion going on outside her house. Always keen to bring people down to earth, she pointed out that it was a big fuss over nothing and that it was just a caterpillar. To add more credibility to her argument, she then picks up a large stone from a nearby garden and promptly crushes the thing under its weight.

'There,' she says finally. 'Show over.'

*

It's a Friday morning in the December of 1997 and my mum and I are in a car being taken over to the studios where Channel 4's early morning TV show, *The Big Breakfast*, is being filmed. My brother Phil is the programme's newsreader and, as a special surprise for one of the episodes shown over Christmas, they have got something special in store for him as a surprise. I am merely here on the trip to keep Mum company and to bathe in my brother's reflected glory. The people from the show haven't given Mum much of an idea about what they have planned, but we know for sure that it will involve her being on TV. My older brother Andy has been on TV a few times (usually for something to do with athletics) and so have I (usually something to do with TV quiz shows). Phil obviously has made being on TV his career. My parents, however, are a different kettle of fish. My mum has never been on TV. Neither has my dad. They have never shown even the remotest interest in being on TV and yet here she is. I ask her why she's agreed to do it and her answer is 'because they asked'. I ask her if she's nervous about being on TV in front of millions of people. She just laughs and says, 'Oh, Michael!' An hour later, she's been sneaked into the studio inside a large purple box decorated like a Christmas present. At the end of Phil's section on camera all attention turns to the box, and my mum leaps out of the box, hands in the air, and like some showbiz know that they will not stand a chance. From the second the whistle is blown the outcome is a foregone conclusion. My mum is so far ahead of the pack that the other mums appear to be left standing. When she crashes through the finishing line and looks around and sees that she has won, she laughs. Big, deep, hearty laughs that make everyone cheering for her smile. She's given a yellow sash and people tell her that she will have to make sure to defend her win next year. She just laughs even louder and says, 'Maybe.'

So I'm eleven (or more possibly twelve) and it's the afternoon, after school, and no one else is in apart from my mum and me. I'm watching the TV in the living room. Who knows what's on? Cartoons? *Blue Peter*? The test card? It doesn't matter. If left to my own devices I will watch the TV even when it's off. Just a blank screen and my own reflection. That's how much I love TV. To me, TV is a place you can escape to that will offer you shelter from the stresses and strains of reality. Enter: my mother. My mother never having grown up with a TV, or even a radio for that matter, can take or leave entertainment at the best of times. To her, at best, it's a nice distraction if there really is nothing else around to distract her. Even so, there's a strict rule in our house concerning the TV: any parent can change channels, at any moment, without consultation. So when Mum walks into the living room and heads for the TV, I know what's coming.

'But I'm watching this.'

'There's something I want to see on BBC2. You can watch TV later.'

'But Mum!'

'But Mum, nothing.' She changes the channels.

'That's not fair.'

She stops and looks at me. 'Not another word.'

I stand up and walk over to her. 'But Mum, I was watching that programme. It won't be on later. It's on now.'

She fixes me with a stare that's a few degrees more serious than the previous one. It says, 'You know I mean it when I say, "Not another word". I mean, not another word or else …'

I say another word. Well, two, actually. 'But Mum …'

I am fully aware that I have now crossed the line. I know that anything that happens in the next fifteen seconds will be my own fault. My mum knows it too. She raises her hand. I don't flinch. She brings it down across my arm. Though it stings, I still don't flinch. All is silent in the room apart from the TV. We stare at each other for what seems like ages. I wonder if I have transgressed another line (a secret line) that will lead her to bring out heavy artillery, the like of which I have never seen. But she doesn't. She just laughs and I laugh too, as I realise that there is no secret line. There is no heavy artillery. There's just me and my mum and a sudden (sad?) realisation that the last of her three sons is no longer just a little boy.

It's the mid-nineties and it's a Saturday afternoon in June, and I've gone round to my parents' house to deliver some news. My dad has gone out, but my mum is in the living room watching an old black and white film, featuring a young Barbara Stanwyck. When I sit myself down on the sofa (an unusual action given that during unsolicited visits it's more usual for us Gayles to stand, making it clear to anyone who's interested that 'we're popping not stopping'), my mum offers me a drink. It has been a long time since I've had a drink at my mum's. Not through choice but rather through circumstance. I live less than ten minutes away by car and so I pop in on them almost every day but rarely stay long enough to require refreshments. Today, however, is different. Today I have news.

'How are you?' asks Mum, bringing in a fizzy drink on a coaster.

'I'm good, thanks, Mum,' I reply. 'In fact I've got some news … Claire and I are getting married.'

My mum raises her eyebrows. It's not a genuine raise of the eyebrows of the surprised or pleased variety, but rather the eyebrow raise of someone who doesn't know how to react to the news. It's as though she's doing an impression of someone reacting to good news in the hope that this will somehow do. I'm not insulted in the least, however. It's not Mum's fault. It's a family thing. The Gayle initial reaction to any kind of news is no reaction at all. It's why we as a people tend to be very calm in a crisis. We don't panic. We just do what needs to be done. We are the worst people in the world with whom to share good news. You get nothing from us at all. That said, we're probably the best people in the world with whom to share bad news because we'd never think for a second to make it about us. We'll listen to your bad news and deal with it accordingly. But we'd never make it into a Big Deal.

I tell my mum not to tell anyone else in the family because I want to tell them myself. Before I've even reached home, I'm fielding phone calls from the rest of my family because Mum has told them the news before me. I don't feel angry or even put out. In fact I'm delighted. This is my mum's surprise and delight in action. This is my mum clapping her hands for joy.

It's a Sunday night in November. I'm nineteen and I'm sitting at home about to make the trip back to university. (It's the first term of the first year of my degree and also the first time I've been home since leaving.) There's no doubt in my mind that I've had a great time. I've been dad's house to pick up my daughter. Mum looks after my kid and my brother's two (a two-year-old girl and a twelve-month-old boy) and it's an arrangement we've had since my daughter was about one. I realise I'm lucky that my mum can help us out like this. I have friends whose parents are no longer alive, or who are too old or live too far away, and I'm always thinking to myself, 'How do these people cope?' But at the same time it can be quite testing having a grandparent involved in childcare. You want them to do things your way because that's how everyone does things these days. They, however, want to do things their way because that's how everyone did things back when they were raising you. And if you try to point out to them that times have changed, they roll their eyes as though 'cot death' is some new-fangled fad brought over from California, or look at you with real hurt in their eyes as though you're covertly criticising the way they brought you up. And then there's the constant stream of surveys. The ones that say your child will be cursed with stupidity if they're not with their parents 24/7; the ones that say that children left in nurseries will be destined for greatness because they're surrounded by children their own age; the ones that say you'd be better off putting your child in front of the TV than handing them over to a grandparent on a regular basis. And you try not to listen to these surveys. But you fail because deep down nights.) As we climb onto the steam train I don't notice if Mum is tired. In fact I don't pay her that much attention at all because I'm distracted by the steam coming from the train and the desperate urge to put my head out of the window to get a better look. In the afternoon, as is the tradition on the Sunday school outing, we go to a nearby village hall for a picnic. My mum has brought a veritable feast. Ham sandwiches with onion (one of my mum's pet hates is bland food), crisps, fruit and a Tupperware container filled with frozen water so that we can make ourselves a drink of ice-cold Ribena. After lunch there are games organised for the kids, and as I prepare for a game of French cricket I notice my mum pulling the blue nylon sleeping bag (the one that my older brothers use when they go camping) out of a large plastic Woolworth's carrier bag. With as little fuss as possible she unfurls the sleeping bag, arranges herself in it and closes her eyes. Though I'm only eight I know that it's not normal for your mum to be taking a nap in a sleeping bag on a Sunday school outing. None of the other mums are doing it. But then again, none of the other mums have just come in from a twelve-hour shift working in a hospital. I'm guessing that if they had, they wouldn't be here at all. They would be asleep in bed and no one would blame them. But my mum's not in bed. She's here with me, napping in a blue nylon sleeping bag on a green outside a village hall, not caring what other people think of her, because that's the kind of mum she is. And I know it's not normal. And I don't really care. I know she's better than normal because she's right here with me.

Out of Time

Mary Loudon

Six in the morning.
Luminous with sunshine borrowed
In advance from another season,
As if the month of May
Held all of June in reserve,
The day is fierce with premature heat.

I am up for a reason.
I have this poem to write
And I not only missed the deadline,
I simply forgot.
Once upon a time I was a writer
Who remembered, at least, to write.
But now, with two children,
A baby due,
And a mind more vulnerable
To the lurch and caprice of each day,
I must, if I am not to fail,

Break in to my former self,
Sneak to my desk
In the hope of recovering an hour
That once belonged to me.

I always used to write at six –
Or run, or swim.
These days, I head for water when children sleep.
The computer stays off.
But to imply such changes are unwelcome
Would dishonour the essential truth –
That I love the present.
Because a life interrupted
– like this –
Is a life transformed.
So I rarely bother with how it was,
Instead content with how it is,
Mundane and sacred, both:
Out of milk; whites on at 60;
My daughters' uncertain thrill when thunder comes
And a blue sky bruises purple …
Exhausting, the tension between the two, sometimes.

*

That I would alter none of it
Is just as well,
For as I head for time alone
And the beginning of a poem,

There are voices:
My daughters,
Their heads inclined,
Conferring soberly in the bathroom.
Something about spiders.

Weeks later,
Poem unwritten,
I lie awake
Considering people without spiders in their bathrooms:
Friends with babies unborn,
Often for years unsought,
Then tirelessly pursued
With all the panic of a frantic search
For recently vanished jewels.
Their hopes not entirely diminished
By cycles of effort unrewarded,
These are people with parents trapped inside them
On permanent standby.

How different things might be
Without my own children
I do not imagine;
Such thoughts lead me always
From dreams of life on a beach
(With work attached)

To death's awful contemplation.
It happens:
A couple I know, their baby died
And they live still; I don't know how.
Sometimes people say of them
What good parents they'd have made.
Extraordinary,
How alchemy goes unnoticed,
And a newborn state is dismissed
If created by a child departed.
Terrible,
When the leaving is so swift
There is no chance to show the world
A transformation undergone –
Love's panorama
Revealed, understood,
And within a missing son's body another world
That endures nonetheless.

*

Suddenly –
My baby is eight weeks old
And I am out of time.
Feeding her at four am
I know I must succumb –
Rising
For tea and the energy
I need to keep my word,

Mary Loudon

I stumble across a birthday party
Taking place at the kitchen table –
My older daughters' work:
Pink plates before dolls,
An elephant with a table napkin.
A laptop – my husband's –
Sits quietly to one side of
Some loud plastic biscuits
And a decorated wooden cake.
I should like really to return to bed
But the light is thickening outside.
I know the weakness inherent
In the way I am about to proceed
But there is no other hour available
To find a poem for months held captive
By a mutinous pregnant body,
So I make a start right here, right now
– Just me, the kettle, the keyboard, the dawn –
Looking up,
From time to time,
At yesterday's party
Left intact by special request.

P.S.

Biographical Notes

Kate Atkinson was born in York and now lives in Edinburgh. Her first novel, *Behind the Scenes at the Museum*, won the Whitbread Book of the Year Award. She is also the author of a collection of short stories, *Not the End of the World*, and of the critically acclaimed novels *Human Croquet* and *Emotionally Weird*. Her bestselling novel, *Case Histories* introduced the character Jackson Brodie and won the Saltire Book of the Year Award and the Prix Westminster. Her most recent book is *One Good Turn*.

Quentin Blake was born in 1932. His professional life started in *Punch* and *The Spectator* and other magazines, and his first children's book was published in 1960. The books he has illustrated, both for children and for adults, number some three hundred and, while his drawings will now forever be associated with the name of Roald Dahl, there have also been memorable and ongoing collaborations with John Yeoman, Joan Aiken, Russell Hoban and Michael Rosen, as well as a sequence of his own picture books, such as *Clown*, *Cockatoos*, *Zagazoo* and *The Green Ship*. In 1999 he was appointed the first Children's Laureate.

Sarah Brown is married to Gordon Brown and is President of the charity PiggyBankKids, which she founded in 2002. PiggyBankKids supports a wide range of charitable projects which create opportunities for children and young people, and has launched the Jennifer Brown Research Fund to seek solutions to pregnancy difficulties and help save newborn lives. Sarah and Gordon live in Fife and London with their sons John and Fraser.

Stephanie Calman created the hit Channel 4 sitcom *Dressing for Breakfast.* She has written for most British newspapers and magazines including the *Daily Telegraph*, the *Observer*, the *Guardian*, *Cosmopolitan*, *GQ* and *Harpers & Queen*, and has been a contributor to a wide variety of radio shows. Stephanie has written four books, *Confessions of a Bad Mother*, *Confessions of a Failed Grown-up*, *Dressing for Breakfast* and *Gentlemen Prefer My Sister*, and is the founder of the seminal and hugely successful www.badmothersclub.com. Stephanie is married with two children. Her hobbies are arguing and lying down.

Caitlin Davies is a mum and freelance journalist in London, writing education features for the *Independent*. She's the author of *Jamestown Blues*, *The Return of El Negro*, *Place of Reeds* and a family saga *Black Mulberries*, to be published summer 2007.

Daisy de Villeneuve has written and illustrated two books – *He Said She Said* which draws upon her life and experiences, and *I Told You So* – both published by Pocko Editions and featuring her trademark style of felt-tip and typewriter. She brought her illustrations to the masses in her October 2003–2004 collaboration with Topshop – her felt-tip girls adorned shoe boxes, underwear and all manner of home wares including bedding and crockery. She also joined forces in 2004 with Nike to customise their Tyvek jackets. Most recently, Daisy has collaborated with Heal's to design a mug for Shelter and with the V&A, producing a limited edition T-shirt inspired by a miniature of Elizabeth I. Her website is www.daisydevilleneuve.com.

Isla Dewar was born in Edinburgh in the golden years before the country went metric and half-crowns and shiny sixpences jingled in your pockets. She worked as a journalist and, finding facts troublesome, switched to fiction. Of her ten novels, many have been bestsellers and have been translated into seventeen languages. Her second book was made into a movie starring Helena

Bonham Carter, *Women Talking Dirty*, with Isla writing the script. She has two sons and lives in Crail, in Fife, with her husband – a cartoonist and illustrator, several cats and a golden retriever.

Mike Gayle is a freelance journalist and author of six bestselling novels: *My Legendary Girlfriend*, *Mr Commitment*, *Turning Thirty*, *Dinner For Two*, *His 'n' Hers* and *Brand New Friend*. His latest novel, *Wish You Were Here*, is out in spring 2007.

Joanne Harris was born in Barnsley in 1964. For fifteen years she taught modern languages at Leeds Grammar School before finally giving up teaching in 2000 to write full time. She is the author of eight novels, including *Chocolat* – which was made into an academy award-nominated movie in 2001, a book of short stories and two cookbooks, *The French Kitchen* and *The French Market*, co-written with Fran Warde. Joanne Harris is married and living in Huddersfield with her husband Kevin and her twelve-year-old daughter, Anouchka.

Shirley Hughes was born and grew up in West Kirby, near Liverpool. She studied at Liverpool Art School and at the Ruskin School of Art in Oxford, before embarking on a career as a freelance illustrator. At first she worked as an interpretive illustrator, but she began to write and design her own picture books when her children were very young. Her first book, *Lucy and Tom's Day*, was published in 1960. Now living in London's Notting Hill, her books have sold over 11 million copies and she is renowned as a champion of children's literature.

Lisa Jewell is the author of six bestselling novels, including *Ralph's Party*, *Thirtynothing* and *Vince & Joy*. She used to be a receptionist until redundancy, a bet and a book deal took her away from all that. She lives in London with her husband and their three-year-old daughter, and if she wasn't a writer she would like to be a midwife. Or maybe a restaurant critic.

Sally Ann Lasson is a freelance journalist and cartoonist. Her cartoon strip, *As If*, appears daily in the *Independent*. She lives in London.

Natasha Law was born and raised in London. She graduated from Camberwell College of Arts in 2000. In the same year she was nominated one of *i-D*'s '200 for 2000'. Since then she's worked as both an artist and a fashion illustrator. Her illustrations are published regularly in *Vogue*, *Gloss*, *Jane*, *Harper's Bazaar* and *The Sunday Times Style* magazine, and her celebrity clientele include Kim Cattrall, Jonny Lee Miller, Betty Jackson, Jo Whiley and the Olsen Twins. Natasha's illustrations are also gracing the pages of Camilla Morton's bestselling book *How to Walk in High Heels*.

Kathy Lette first achieved *succès de scandale* as a teenager with the novel *Puberty Blues*, which became a major film. After several years as a singer in a rock band and a newspaper columnist in Sydney and New York (collected in the book *Hit and Ms*) and as a television sitcom writer for Columbia Pictures in Los Angeles, her novels – *Girls' Night Out*, *The Llama Parlour*, *Foetal Attraction*, *Mad Cows* (made into a film starring Joanna Lumley and Anna Friel), *Altar Ego*, *Nip 'n' Tuck*, *Dead Sexy* and *How to Kill Your Husband and Other Handy Household Hints* – all became international bestsellers. Lette is now published in seventeen languages, in over one hundred countries of the world.

Mary Loudon is the author of *Relative Stranger; Secrets and Lives, Middle England Revealed; Revelations, The Clergy Questioned;* and *Unveiled, Nuns Talking*. All four books were published to enormous critical acclaim: *Relative Stranger* has been sold worldwide. An experienced broadcaster and critic, Mary has won four writing prizes, contributed to five anthologies and has been a Whitbread Prize judge. She lives in Oxfordshire and mid-Wales with her husband and three daughters.

Gil McNeil is the bestselling author of *The Only Boy for Me*, *Stand by your Man*, *In the Wee Small Hours* and *Divas Don't Knit*. She helps run the charity PiggyBankKids, and lives in Canterbury with her son. She has edited previous PiggyBankKids anthologies *Journey to the Sea*, *Magic* and *Summer Magic*.

Santa Montefiore was born in 1970, grew up on a farm in Hampshire and was educated at Sherborne School for Girls. She read Spanish and Italian at Exeter University and spent much of the 90s in Buenos Aires, where her mother grew up. She converted to Judaism in 1998 and married historian Simon Sebag Montefiore in the Liberal Jewish Synagogue in London. She is the author of seven books, including most recently *The Sea of Lost Love*. They live with their two children, Lily and Sasha, in London.

John O'Farrell is an author of a number of bestselling books including *The Best A Man Can Get* and *May Contain Nuts*. A former scriptwriter for *Spitting Image* and *Smith and Jones*, he now regularly appears on such shows as *Have I Got News For You* and *Grumpy Old Men*. He wrote a humorous column in the *Guardian* for five years and recently founded the comedy website www.newsbiscuit.com

Shyama Perera is a journalist and writer. Her books are *Haven't Stopped Dancing Yet*, *Bitter Sweet Symphony*, *Do the Right Thing* and *Taking Precautions*. She lives in London with her daughters.

Gervase Phinn taught in a range of schools for fourteen years until, in 1984, he became General Adviser for Language Development in Rotherham. Four years later he was appointed Senior General Inspector for English and Drama with North Yorkshire County Council and was subsequently made Principal Adviser for the county. He has published collections of his own plays, poetry and stories and has contributed to several anthologies. Gervase Phinn is probably best known for his bestselling autobiographical novels: *The Other Side of the Dale*, *Over Hill and Dale*, *Head Over Heels in the Dales*, *Up and Down in the Dales* and *A Wayne in a Manger*.

Justine Picardie is a journalist and novelist who lives in London with her husband and two sons. She is the author of *If the Spirit Moves You*, *Wish I May* and *My Mother's Wedding Dress.* A former features editor of *Vogue*, she is now a columnist for the *Sunday Telegraph* and *Harper's Bazaar*. Her latest novel, *Daphne*, will be published in 2007.

Rosamunde Pilcher was born in Cornwall in 1924. She spent her childhood there, but her teenage years were wartime years and she ended the war in Trincomalee, in what is now in Sri Lanka. Her writing career began with short stories, and her first novels were published by Mills & Boon, and Collins. It was not until she was sixty that she wrote *The Shell Seekers* which became a bestseller.

Now retired, Rosamunde is much involved with her children and grandchildren. She lives near Dundee with her husband, two dachshunds, and a son and his wife just 'doon the road'.

Charles M. Schulz was born in 1922. His fascination with comic strips began early, reading the Sunday comics from four different newspapers with his father each week. On 2 October 1950, 'Peanuts' debuted in seven newspapers. Fifty years later, 'Peanuts' was appearing in over 2,600 newspapers worldwide and Charles M. Schulz had long become a household name. Unlike many cartoonists, he drew every comic strip without the assistance of an art staff. He also wrote the scripts for the 'Peanuts' television specials, which garnered five Emmy Awards. On 12 February 2000, Charles Schulz died of complications from colon cancer. It was only hours before his last original strip was to appear in Sunday papers. He is survived by his wife, Jeannie, his five children, two stepchildren and their families.

Posy Simmonds was born in 1945 and grew up in Berkshire. She studied graphic design at the Central School of Art in London. She has contributed to a variety of magazines and journals, including *The Times*, the *Sun* and *Cosmopolitan*. In 1972, she created a popular cartoon strip about a middle-class couple, George and Wendy Weber, for the *Guardian*. She has also produced graphic novels, including *True Love* and *Gemma Bovery*, has written and illustrated children's books, and has created *Lulu and the Flying Babies* and the very popular *Fred* – the film version of which was nominated for an Oscar. She was named Cartoonist of the Year in 1980 and 1981. Her most recent books are *Lavender* and *Baker Cat*, for children, and *Literary Life*. Posy Simmonds lives in London.

Alexander McCall Smith was born in Zimbabwe and educated there and in Scotland. He is Emeritus Professor of Medical Law at the University of Edinburgh and is a former member of a number of national and international bodies concerned with bioethics. His books include works on medical law, criminal law and philosophy, as well as numerous books for children, collections of short stories and novels. *The No.1 Ladies' Detective Agency* has been translated into over thirty languages and has sold over 12 million copies worldwide.

Meera Syal co-writes and is a cast member of the popular BBC television comedy series *Goodness Gracious Me*, and also works as a journalist. Her childhood experiences of growing up in a small mining community provided the background to her first novel, *Anita and Me*, which was shortlisted for the *Guardian* Fiction Prize and won a Betty Trask Award. Her second novel was *Life Isn't All Ha Ha Hee Hee*. Meera was awarded an MBE in 1997 and won the Media Personality of the Year Award at the Commission for Racial Equality's annual Race in the Media Awards (2000), as well as the EMMA (BT Ethnic and Multicultural Media Award) for Media Personality of the Year in 2001.

Penny Vincenzi began her career as a junior secretary for *Vogue* and *Tatler*. She later worked as fashion and beauty editor on magazines such as *Woman's Own*, *Nova* and *Honey*, before becoming contributing editor for *Cosmopolitan*. She is the author of two humorous books and eleven novels. Penny Vincenzi is married with four daughters.

PiggyBankKids is a charity which creates opportunities for children and young people who would otherwise miss out. An umbrella charity, running a number of projects, we often work in partnership with other charities. All our work is in the UK. PiggyBankKids' work includes:

The Jennifer Brown Research Fund

Led by Professor Andrew Calder, a talented and dedicated team of scientists are advancing four pioneering research projects that are making real progress towards resolving some of the life threatening complications that can arise during pregnancy. The fund finances four separate research projects – looking at pre-eclampsia, early labour problems, curing blindness in premature babies and reducing incidences of brain damage in premature babies.

The Fife Appeal

The Jennifer Brown Research Fund also supports smaller innovative support schemes implemented by Fife maternity health professionals. These include Play Away, a project based in Dunfermline supporting isolated younger families, and the Maternity Bus, a service which collects teenage girls from their homes and offers parenthood teaching sessions on the bus.

Other charities we support:

Mentoring

PiggyBankKids supports a wide range of amazing children's charities providing opportunities for vulnerable young people around the UK. Chance UK seeks to provide an early and transforming intervention in vulnerable children's lives so that, together with their families, they can build a brighter future. It provides targeted solution-focused mentoring for children aged five to eleven, based on individual needs. To support the work of mentoring charities we published *Moving On Up* in 2002, where famous people wrote about the mentors who had most influenced their lives. Free copies of *Moving On Up* were sent to every state and independent secondary school in the UK.

Competing

Special Olympics is an international non-profit organisation dedicated to empowering individuals with intellectual disabilities to become physically fit, productive and respected members of society through sports training and competition. In 2005 we published *Journey to the Sea*, a collection of new fiction and travel writing, to support the work of Special Olympics Great Britain.

Training

Youth Culture Television (YCTV) Foundation, established in 1994, is an educational charity that uses the medium of TV and programme production to advance the skills and personal development of socially excluded young people.

The Big Night In

To support all our projects, the Big Night In was devised for those who want to do something for charity but don't have time to train for a marathon or walk the Great Wall of China. Money raised during the Big Night In goes directly to projects ranging from the Jennifer Brown Research Fund, to mentoring and family support services and charities focusing on improving sports provision for vulnerable young people.

For further information please contact:
Joe Hewitt
Project Co-ordinator
PiggyBankKids
16 Lincoln's Inn Fields
London WC2A 3ED
020 7936 1293
You can read more about PiggyBankKids projects at:
www.piggybankkids.org